Part one
CALLIGRAPHY

Caroline Young

Designed by Jane Felstead

Consultant : Susan Hufton
(Fellow of the Society of Scribes)

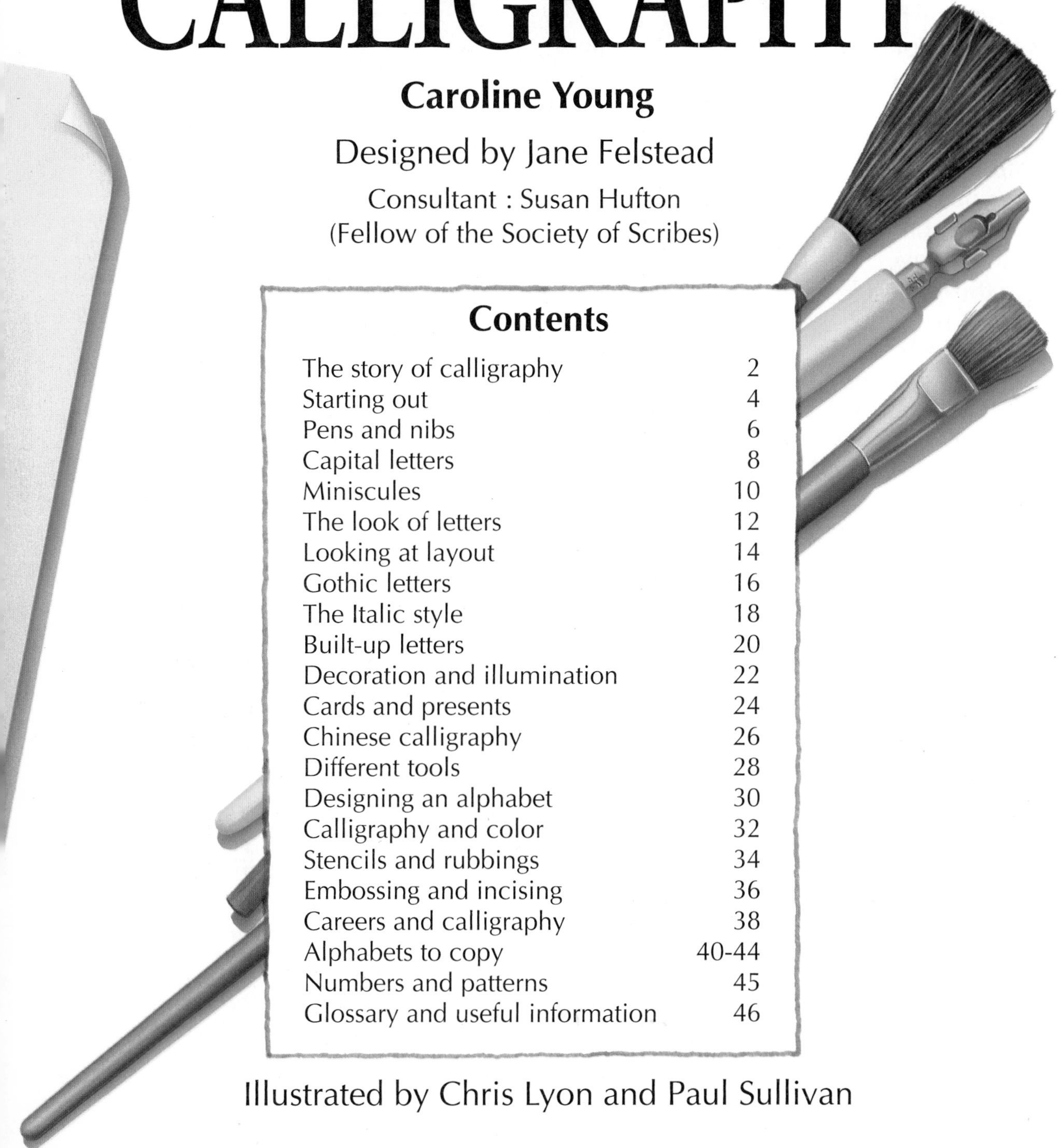

Contents

The story of calligraphy	2
Starting out	4
Pens and nibs	6
Capital letters	8
Miniscules	10
The look of letters	12
Looking at layout	14
Gothic letters	16
The Italic style	18
Built-up letters	20
Decoration and illumination	22
Cards and presents	24
Chinese calligraphy	26
Different tools	28
Designing an alphabet	30
Calligraphy and color	32
Stencils and rubbings	34
Embossing and incising	36
Careers and calligraphy	38
Alphabets to copy	40-44
Numbers and patterns	45
Glossary and useful information	46

Illustrated by Chris Lyon and Paul Sullivan

Calligraphy by Susan Hufton
Additional calligraphy by Solus Solou

SCHOLASTIC INC.
New York Toronto London Auckland Sydney
Mexico City New Delhi Hong Kong Buenos Aires

what is calligraphy?

Calligraphy is the art of beautiful writing. The basic techniques of the calligrapher are the same today as they were centuries ago. Here you can see the development of calligraphy from the earliest forms of writing. You will find out how to write some of the calligraphy styles shown here later in this book.

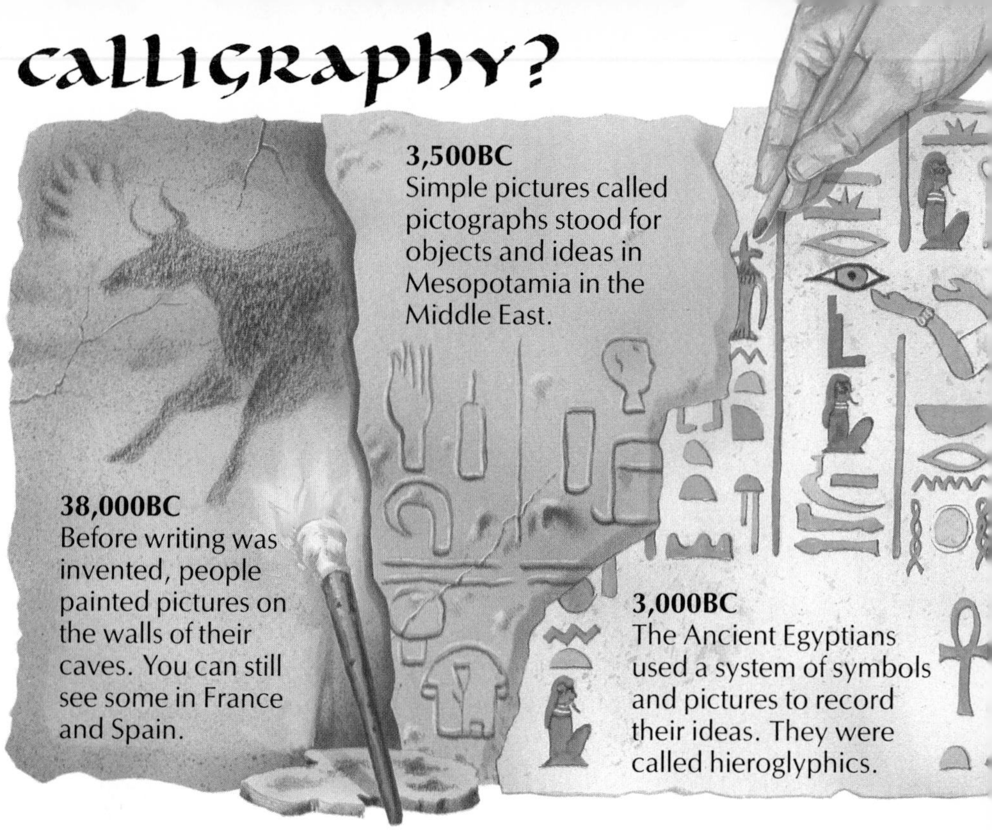

3,500BC
Simple pictures called pictographs stood for objects and ideas in Mesopotamia in the Middle East.

38,000BC
Before writing was invented, people painted pictures on the walls of their caves. You can still see some in France and Spain.

3,000BC
The Ancient Egyptians used a system of symbols and pictures to record their ideas. They were called hieroglyphics.

1st century AD
The Ancient Romans adapted the Greeks' alphabet to produce their own 23 capital letters (see page 8). They carved, or incised, them into stone and marble.

The Romans used a broad nib, held at a constant angle, to write in books. This made simpler capitals, called Rustics. These were the first calligraphy letters.

ONVTRIX
LAMATRES
ADECORIS
VSILLI

Rustic capitals

1st to 10th centuries AD
In some countries, the letters J, U and W were added to the 23 Roman capitals to make a 26 letter alphabet.

J U
W

Around the 6th century, monks used a calligraphy style called Uncials to write beautifully decorated religious books. You can learn how to write Uncials on page 12.

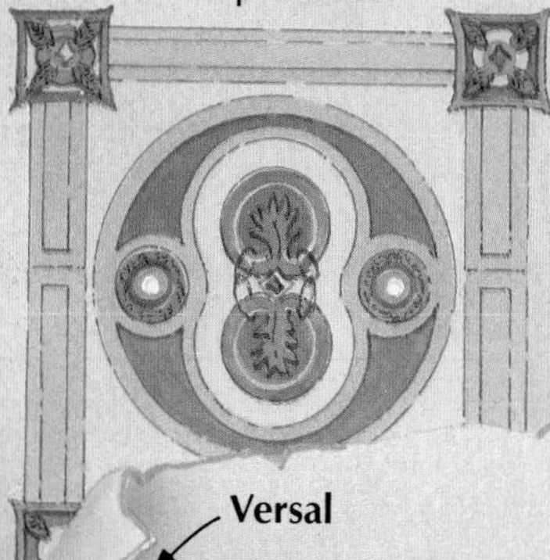

Uncials

Sicut nouit me pater
et ego agnosco patrem
Et animam meam pono
pro quibu...

Versal

Adquem autem angel
adextrıſ meıſ quoadu
ſcabellum pedum tu
amm...

Carolingian minuscules

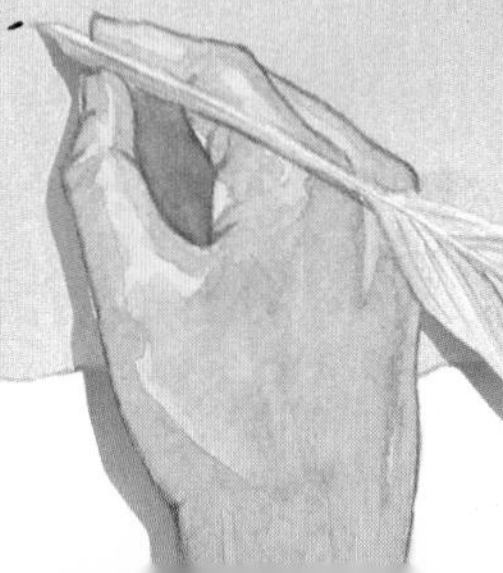

By the 9th century, most people were using small letters, or minuscules, as well as capitals. The most common style was called the Carolingian minuscule (see page 40).

Capital letters built up with several pen strokes were often used with minuscules. They were called Versals (see page 20).

2,500BC
The first real writing, called cuneiform, was invented in Mesopotamia. Marks made in clay with a wedge-shaped tool stood for sounds. These made up words.

1,500BC
At this time, the Chinese began using a complicated script with more than 1500 characters. Each character stood for a whole idea. You can find out how to write some on page 27.

1,000BC
Sea-traders called Phoenicians used an alphabet of 22 letters. They spread this alphabet to many Mediterranean countries.

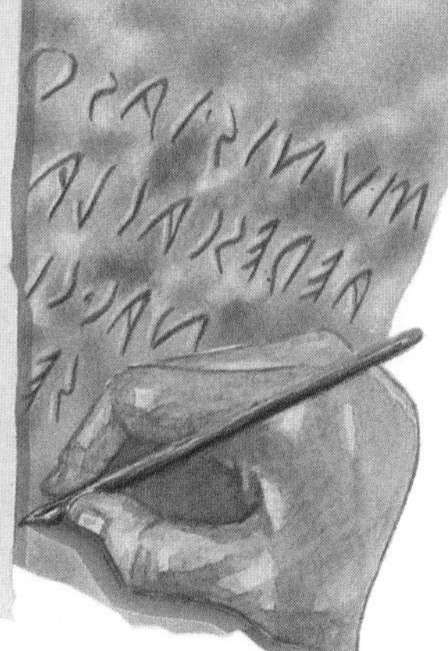

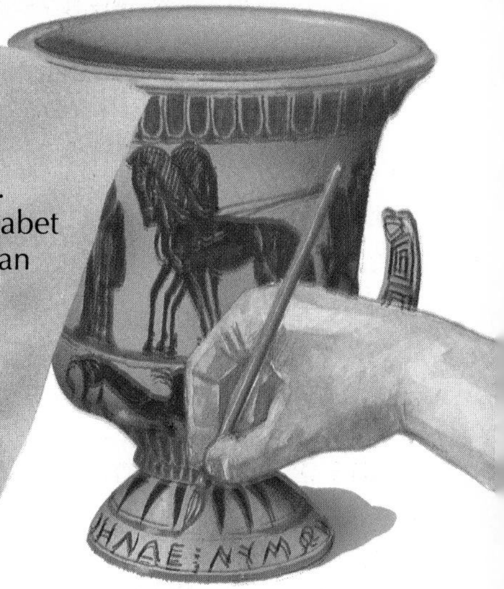

500BC
The Ancient Greeks adapted some of the Phoenician alphabet and added some vowels (A,E,I and O) as well.

13th-15th century AD
To fit more onto a line, people started writing narrower letters closer together. This gradually developed into the Gothic style you can see on page 16.

Tunc det ei eps iurgam pac toralem dicens.

Around the end of the 1400s, people wanted a writing style that was simpler than Gothic. Scholars in Italy developed Italics, which could be beautiful calligraphy or just elegant handwriting (see pages 18-19).

Italic handwriting

Signor, che parti et tempri gli elementi,

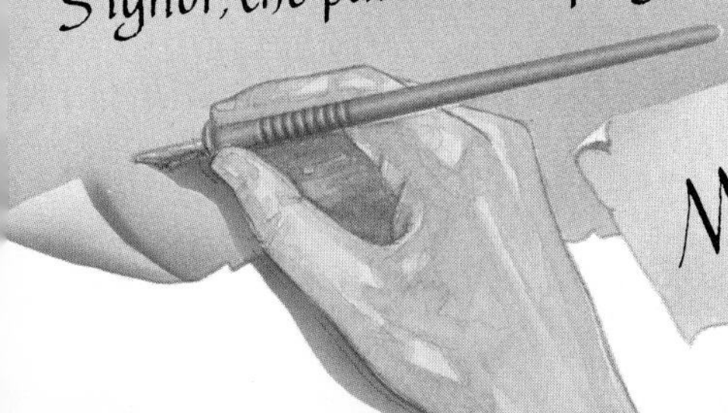

15th-19th century AD
In 1450, the first printing press was set up in Germany. Its letters were based on the Gothic calligraphy style.

und vorcht scheidē vō euch
nicht wo ir wandett · wī

Gothic print

Once books were printed and not written by hand, calligraphy became less important. People just used beautiful writing for their everyday handwriting.

Today
Around 1900, the scholar Edward Johnston revived the art of calligraphy. He taught historical styles and one he developed himself based on a 10th century manuscript. It was called Foundational.

10th century letters

angeli

angels

Foundational letters

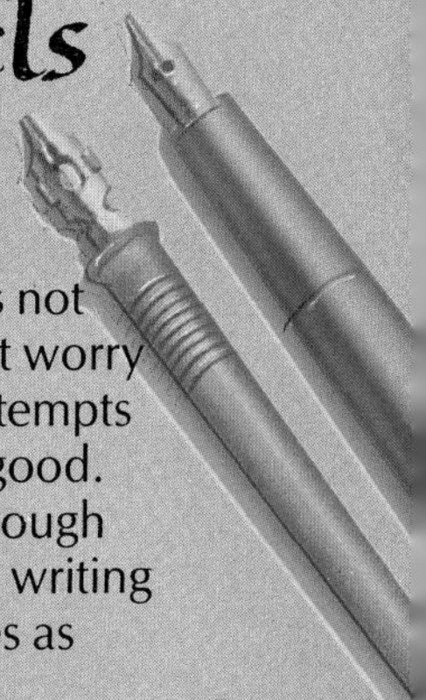

Calligraphy is not easy, so don't worry if your first attempts are not very good. As you go through this book, try writing as many styles as you can.

STARTING OUT

Below is the basic equipment you need to start doing calligraphy. You can try the main techniques using the simple things on page 5. There are details about buying different kinds of calligraphy pens and nibs on pages 6 and 50.

Basic equipment

You can buy all these things from a good art supply store.

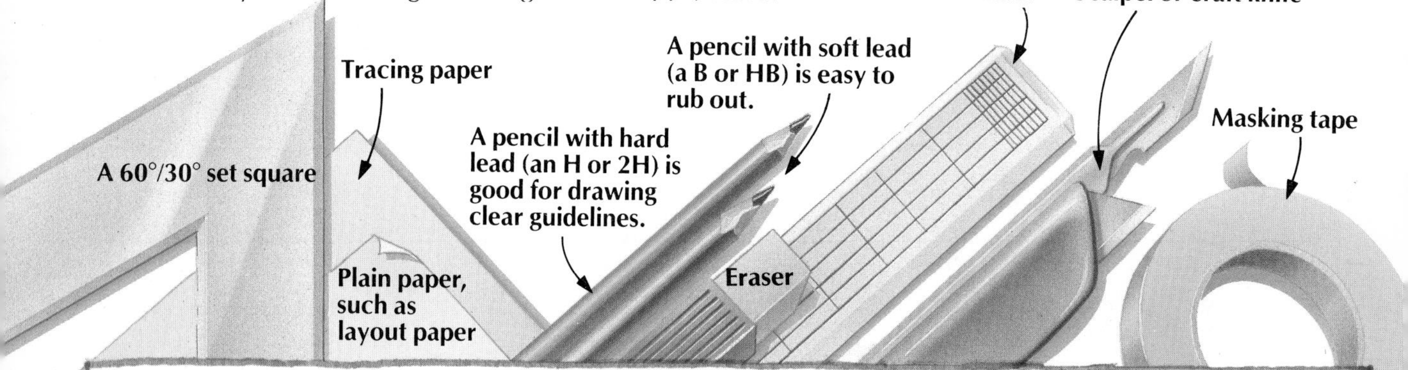

Ruler
Scalpel or craft knife
Tracing paper
A pencil with soft lead (a B or HB) is easy to rub out.
Masking tape
A pencil with hard lead (an H or 2H) is good for drawing clear guidelines.
A 60°/30° set square
Plain paper, such as layout paper
Eraser

Getting ready

Most calligraphers prefer to write on a sloping surface, such as a drawing board. Writing on a flat surface can make the ink flood out of your pen.

Try sticking a sheet of paper to the back of a tray. Rest one edge of a tray on your knees and lean the other against the edge of a table.

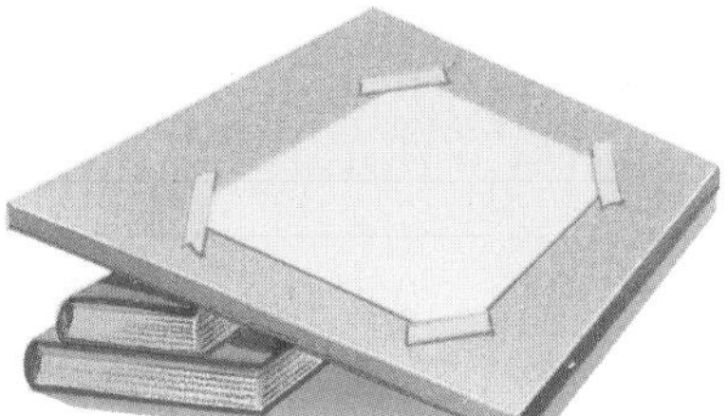

Lean a board against a pile of heavy books on a table for a more stable writing surface.

You could make a drawing board from a piece of wood from around your home, or plywood from a lumber yard. It should be at least 60cm long, 42cm wide and 1cm thick.

Writing hints

Here are some hints to help you produce better calligraphy.

- Sit near a window if possible. If you need a desk lamp, it should shine over the opposite shoulder to your writing hand.
- Tape several sheets of paper under the sheet you are going to write on. They will act as a pad.
- Tape another sheet of paper over your work to keep it clean. Move your worksheet up to start each new line.
- Sit up straight, with both feet flat on the floor as shown in the picture on the right. Keep the part of your arm from your wrist to your elbow on the board as you write.

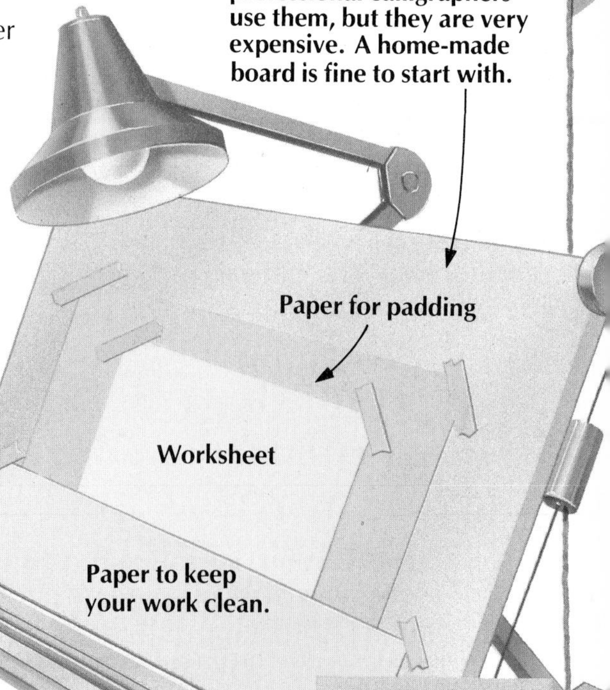

This is a parallel motion drawing board. Many professional calligraphers use them, but they are very expensive. A home-made board is fine to start with.
Paper for padding
Worksheet
Paper to keep your work clean.

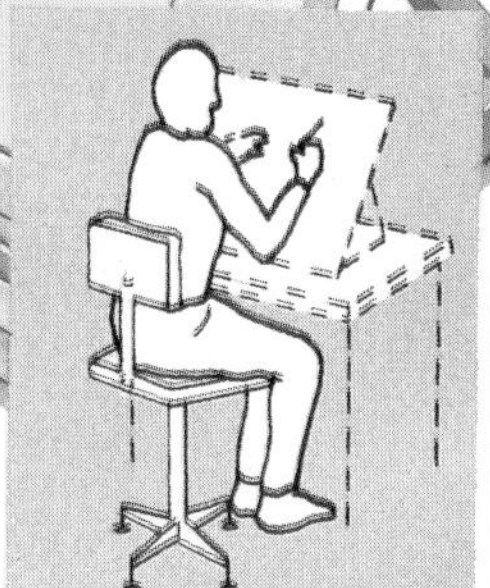

The correct angle

Calligraphers write with a broad nib held at a constant angle. In this book, pictures like the one on the right show you the angle to hold your nib at as you write each calligraphy style.

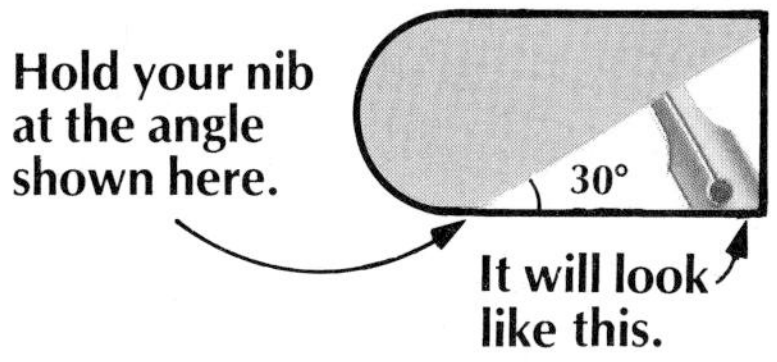
Hold your nib at the angle shown here.
30°
It will look like this.

Thick and thin

When you write like this with a broad nib you will find that your pen makes thick and thin strokes. Try it yourself using a a homemade pen or double-pencils (see page 51).

Cardboard pen

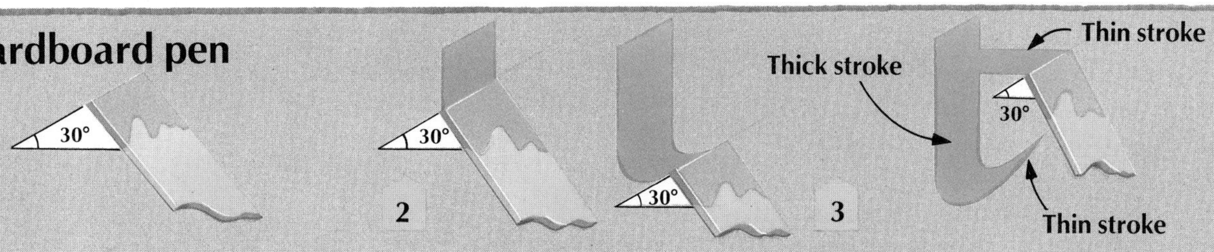
30°
Thick stroke
Thin stroke
Thin stroke

1. Dip a strip of cardboard about 3cm wide into some ink. Hold it at a 30° angle as shown above.
2. Holding your cardboard pen at the same angle all the time, write the letter 't'.
3. Your wide 'nib' will make some strokes thin and some strokes thick.

Tip

Homemade pens are ideal for doing large lettering on posters. On pages 58-59 you will find ideas which show you how to decorate giftwrap using pens you have made.

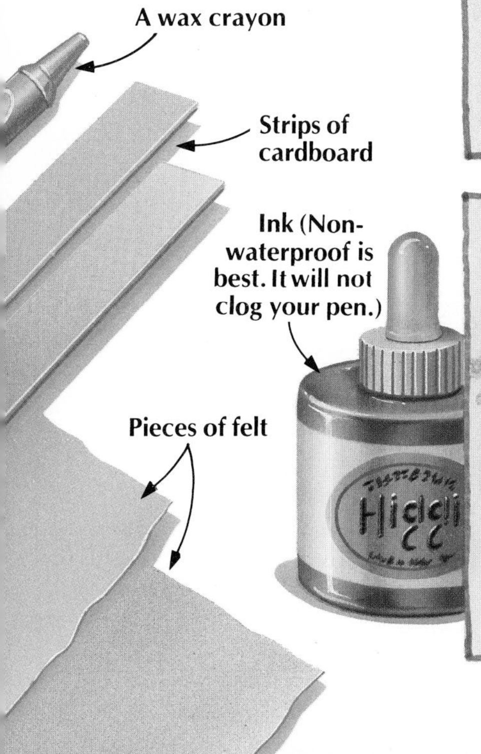
A wax crayon
Strips of cardboard
Ink (Non-waterproof is best. It will not clog your pen.)
Pieces of felt

Felt pens

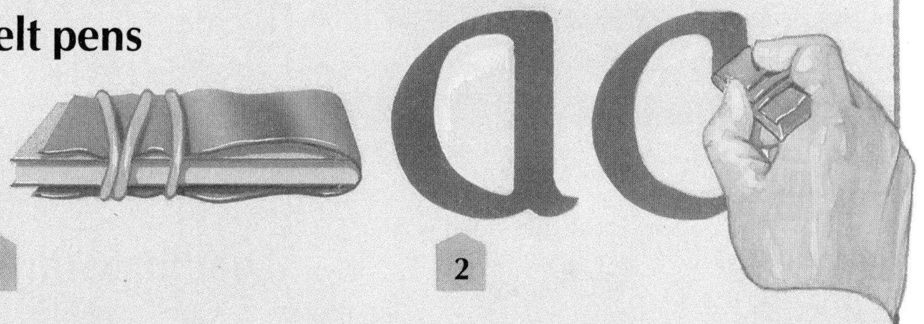

1. Wrap a felt strip about 2cm by 6cm around some stiff cardboard the same size. Secure it with a rubber band.
2. Dip the covered end of your pen into some ink. Holding the pen at a constant 30° angle, write a selection of letters.

Wax crayon

1. Rub a piece of wax crayon until one side is flattened. This makes your broad writing-edge.
2. Hold the crayon between your thumb and forefinger at a 30° angle and write any word.

Pens and Nibs

Most calligraphy written on paper is done with an ink-filled pen. However, felt-tip calligraphy pens from a stationer's or a brush and paint can be used for the projects in the second part of this book.

Choosing your pen

There are two types of calligraphy pen. They are dip pens and fountain pens with calligraphy nibs.

Dip pens

Dip pens have three parts: a nib, a pen-holder and a reservoir to hold ink. Each part is inexpensive to buy and easy to replace or change. You may have to go to an art shop to get one.

Nibs are available in ten different widths. The widest, marked 0 or 1, are best to start with. If you are left-handed, you will need a nib called a left oblique nib.

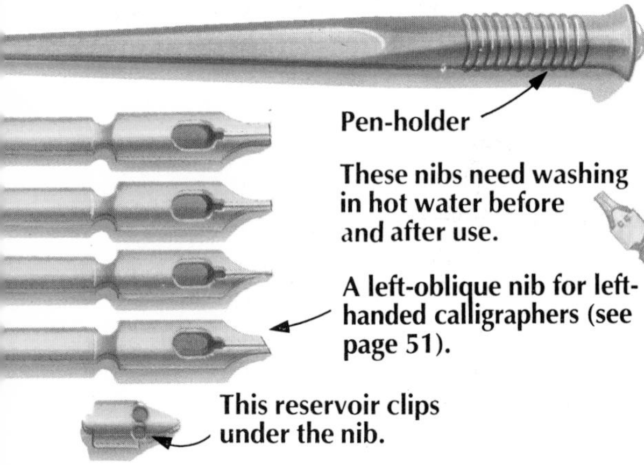

Pen-holder
These nibs need washing in hot water before and after use.
A left-oblique nib for left-handed calligraphers (see page 51).
This reservoir clips under the nib.

Fountain pens

Fountain pens have a supply of ink inside the pen. They are either refilled with ink from a bottle or with replaceable cartridges.

Many art shops sell fountain pens with wide nibs for calligraphy. It is expensive to replace broken nibs and the nib sizes available can be limited, however.

Assembling a dip pen

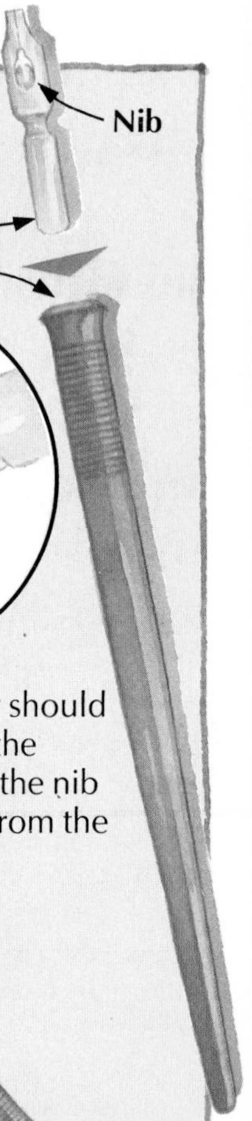

Nib
Tongue
Groove

1 The open end of the pen-holder has a circular groove. Slide the long 'tongue' of the nib into it.

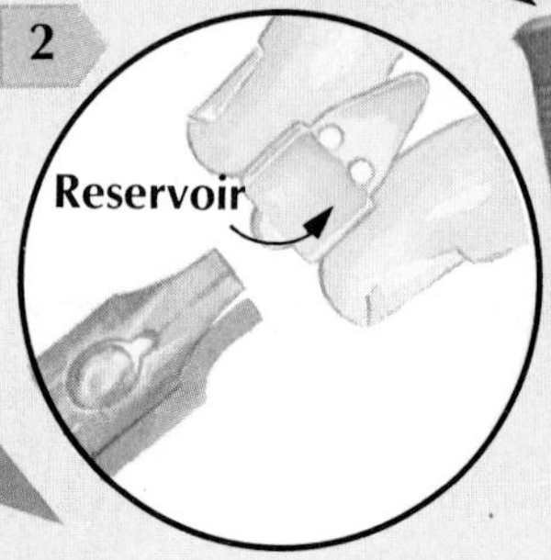

Reservoir

2 Slide the reservoir on to the under side of the nib. Squeeze the small tags until it clips on firmly.

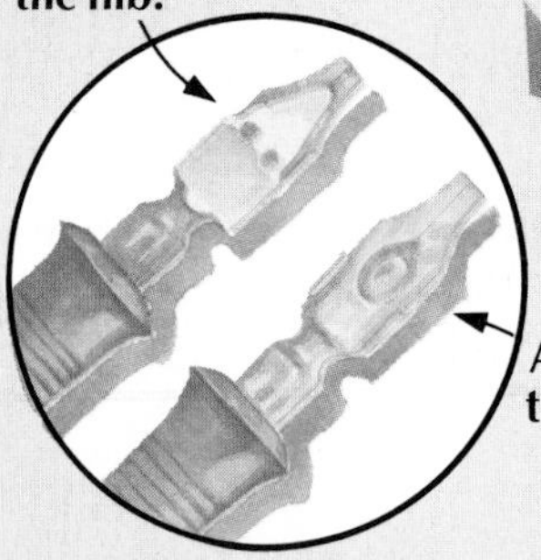

Underneath the nib.
Above the nib.

3 The reservoir should be touching the underside of the nib about 2mm from the tip.

Loading with ink

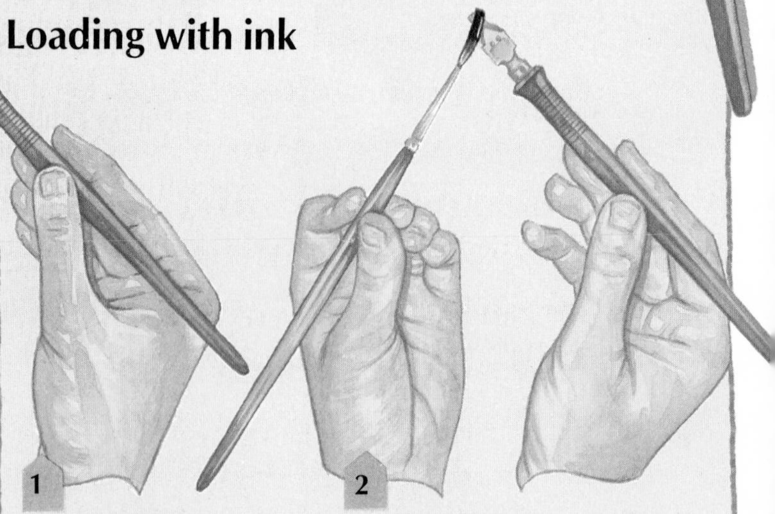

1 To load a pen like this one, turn it so that the reservoir is facing upwards. Hold it so that the nib end of the pen-holder is higher.

2 Dip a small paint brush in ink*. Gently wipe the ink onto the nib by moving the brush downwards. Repeat this until the ink flows into the reservoir.

* Remember to use non-waterproof ink

Writing with your pen

You might find writing with an ink-filled calligraphy pen takes some practice. To get started, make each of the pen-stroke patterns shown below. Follow the arrows and try to keep your pen angle constant as you write.

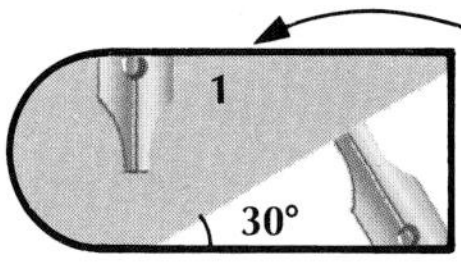

This number tells you what size nib to use.

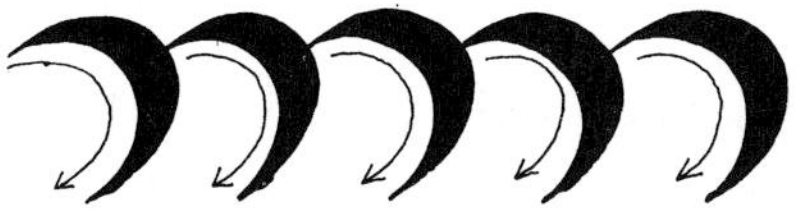

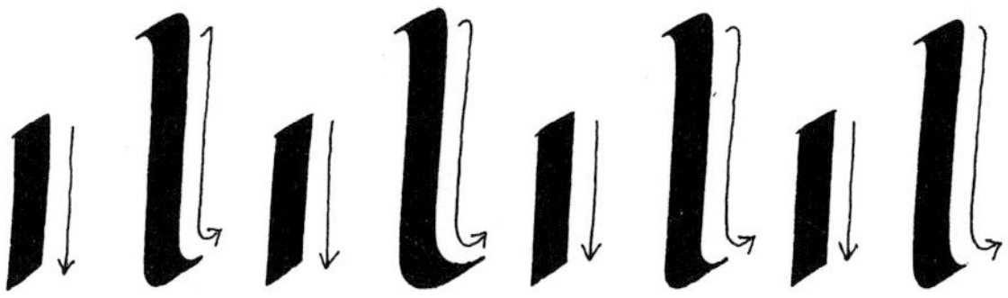

Take the nib off the page between these strokes.

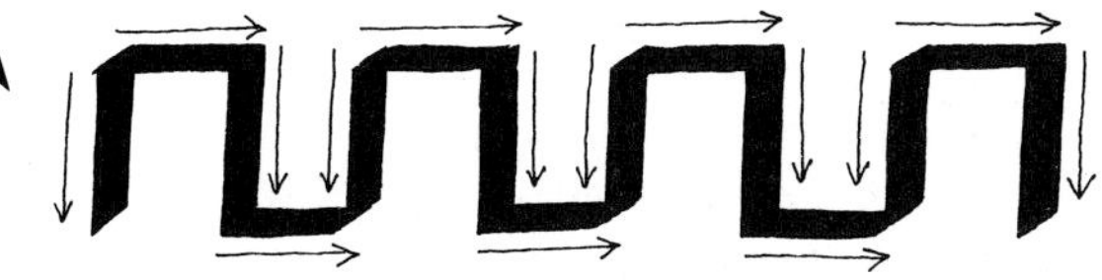

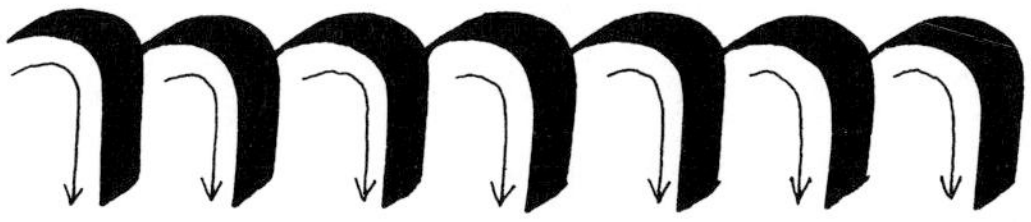

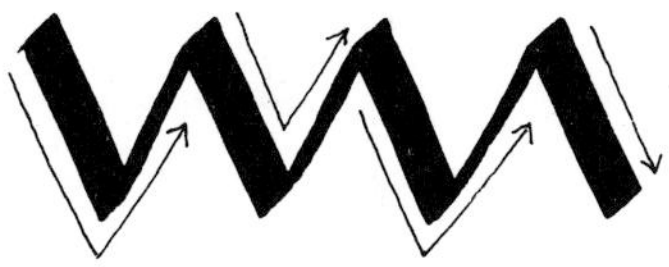

This time, take the nib off the page and draw the second stroke towards you.

Making letters

Calligraphy letters are not written with one continuous pen stroke, like ordinary handwriting. They are made up of several strokes and you take the pen off the paper between them.

Here, two curved strokes make a letter 'O'.

This 'S' is made up of three different strokes.

This calligraphy 'W' has four separate strokes.

You will find out exactly how every letter in the alphabet is formed in each calligraphy style on the pages ahead.

Pen problems

Here are some of the problems you may come across when you first start writing with a calligraphy pen. Possible solutions to them are shown here, too.

Ink is not flowing

- Wash the nib in hot water, it could be greasy. Dry it with a tissue.
- Check the reservoir tabs are not too tight.

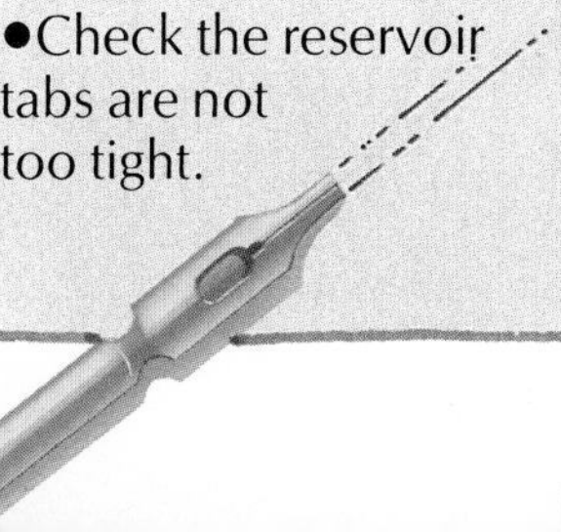

Ink is blobby

- Check that the ink has flowed into the reservoir.
- See if the reservoir is too far from the nib.

Strokes are ragged

- Check that the full width of nib is making contact with the paper.

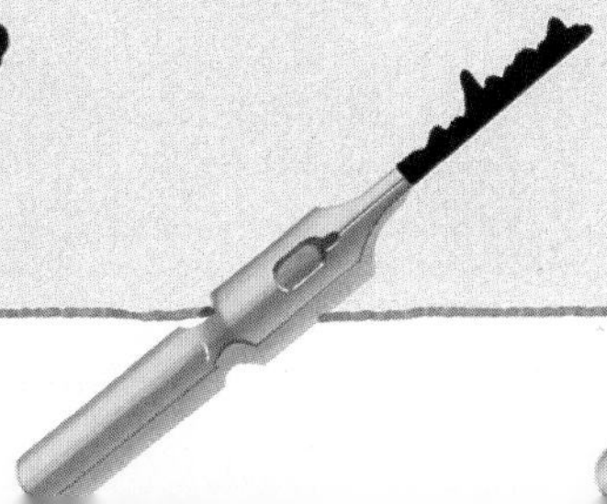

Split strokes

- Make sure you are not pressing too hard, forcing the two parts of the nib to splay apart.

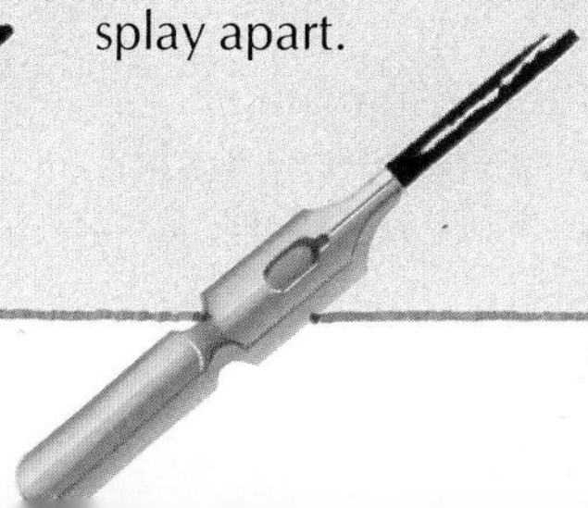

CAPITAL LETTERS

The 26 letters used in most Western languages are called roman letters. They can be written in many different styles. Their basic shapes are adapted from 23 capital letters, or majuscules, used by the Ancient Romans (see page 2). Small letters, or minuscules, developed several centuries later.

Skeleton capitals

The capital letters the Romans used were all based on a grid. They were also divided into groups of letters with similar shapes.

Here you can see them in their groups. They are shown in their simplest form, called a skeleton.

How to write them

1. Fit a medium nib, such as a 3½, into your calligraphy pen and load it with ink. Try some of the practice strokes from page 9 to 'warm up'.

2. Put tracing paper over each grid in turn. Make the strokes of each skeleton letter, following the direction of the arrows.

Checkpoints

- Remember to take your pen off the paper between strokes.
- Check the pen angle of each letter before you start.
- Check that your finished letters look like those on page 40.

Narrow letters | **Round letters** | **Rectangular letters** | **Diagonal letters**

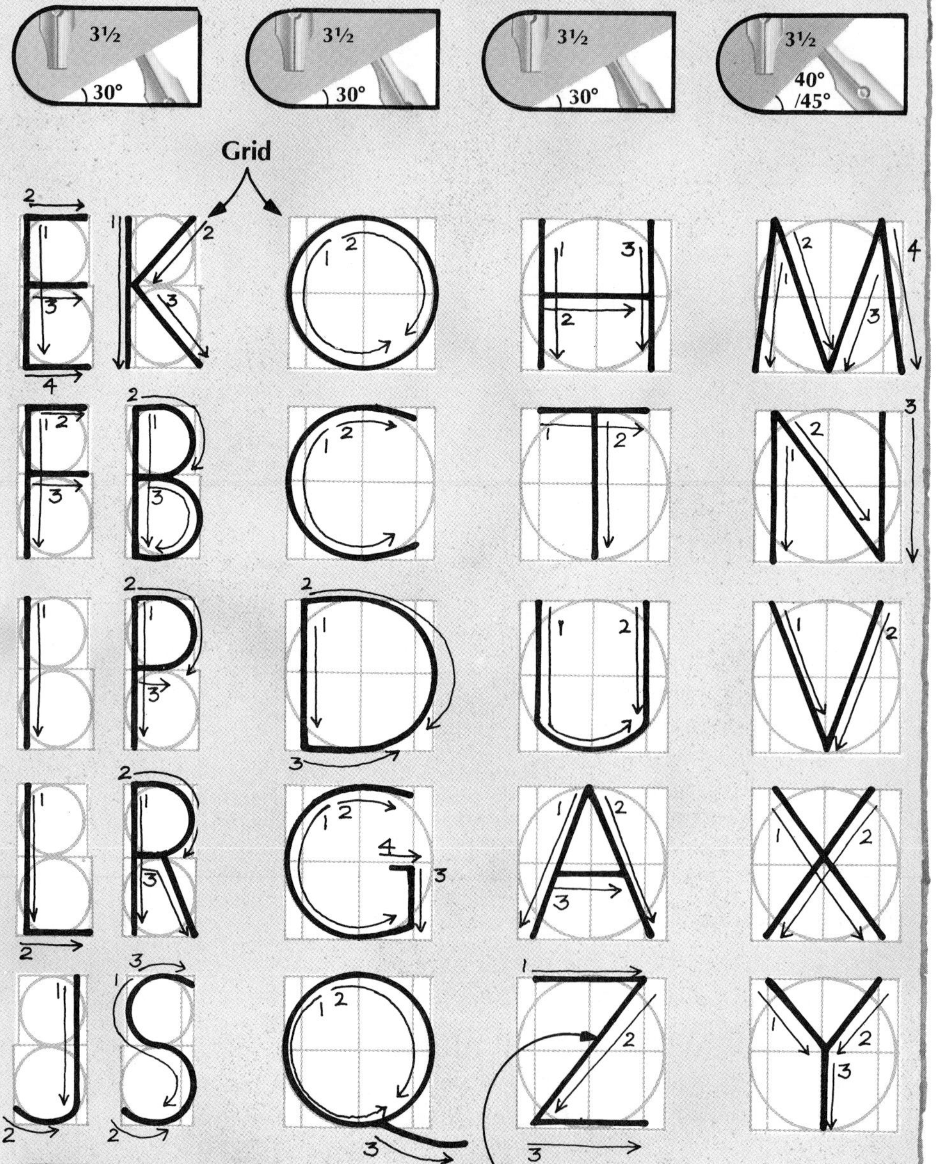

3½
30°
3½
30°
3½
30°
3½
40° /45°
Grid

Tip Try writing the letters again with a thicker nib such as a 1. You will see more difference between thick and thin strokes.

Hold the pen parallel to the bottom line of the grid for this stroke.

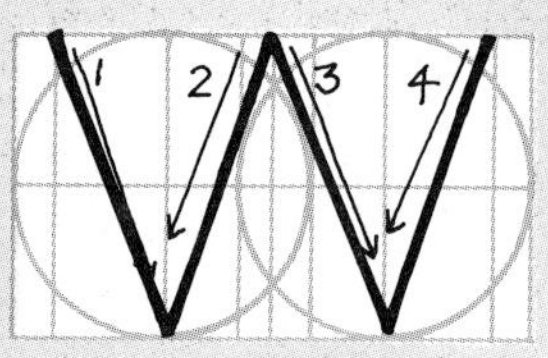

Straight lines

It is easier to write calligraphy between two parallel pencil guidelines. To make sure they start straight, align side A of your set square with the edge of your paper. as shown on the right. Draw a pencil line along side B. Move your set square down and draw another guideline. Use your ruler to lengthen them.

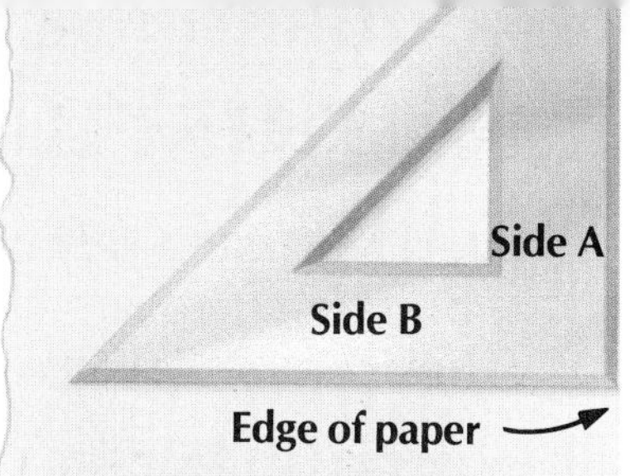

Side A
Side B
Edge of paper

Check your spacing

1 It is important to leave an even amount of space between letters in calligraphy. Rule enough pairs of lines 1 cm apart to write your name and address. Leave ½ cm between each pair.

2 Using the nib size and pen angles on page 8, write your name and address between the guidelines. Try and keep an equal space between letters.

3 Lightly shade in the area between letters with a pencil. Stand back and see whether the shaded areas look roughly the same size. With practice, you should be able to judge the right spacing just by looking.

Leave more space between two letters with vertical strokes.

ANNA POULIN
8, RUE DU PONT
MA

If you make a mistake, gently scrape it off the paper with a scalpel.

Capital calligraphy

When you feel ready, try using Roman capitals for a special piece of work. You could buy a greeting card with no message inside it and write your own.

GOOD
LUCK
love
Maria

Serifs

The picture below shows some letters carved into stone by the Ancient Romans. The decorative 'feet' on the end of the letter strokes are called serifs.

In stone, they were formed by the mason's chisel. In calligraphy, serifs can either be built into the pen stroke or added on afterwards.

This serif is a small hook before the stroke.

These serifs are straight strokes added onto the letter.

A
Serifs

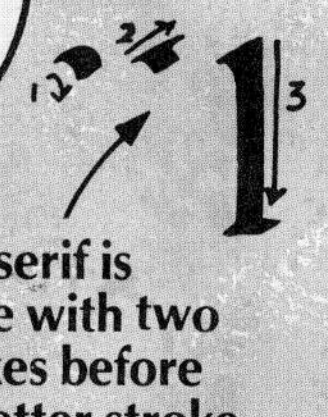

1
2
3

This serif is made with two strokes before the letter stroke.

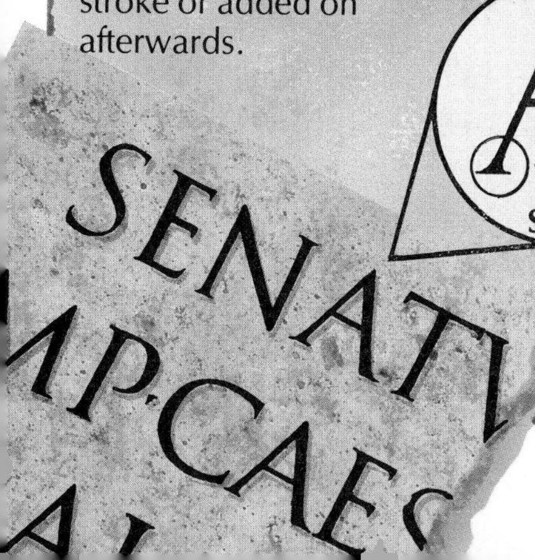

SENAT
P.CAES

Sans serif

Letters that do not have serifs are called sans serif. This means 'without serif' in French.

With your calligraphy pen, write the same word three times.

ROM

Now try adding a different sort of serif to the letters of each word. Stand back, and see how different the letters look.

ROM

ROM

Tip Once you feel confident about writing these letters, try adding serifs as you write each one. This might take some practice.

Minuscules

Here you can find out how small letters, or minuscules, are formed in calligraphy. They can be written in many different styles. Once you have learned some basic facts about them, you should be able to master any calligraphy style.

Skeleton shapes

Minuscules, like capitals, divide into groups of letters with similar shapes. It is a good idea to learn them in their groups in skeleton form.

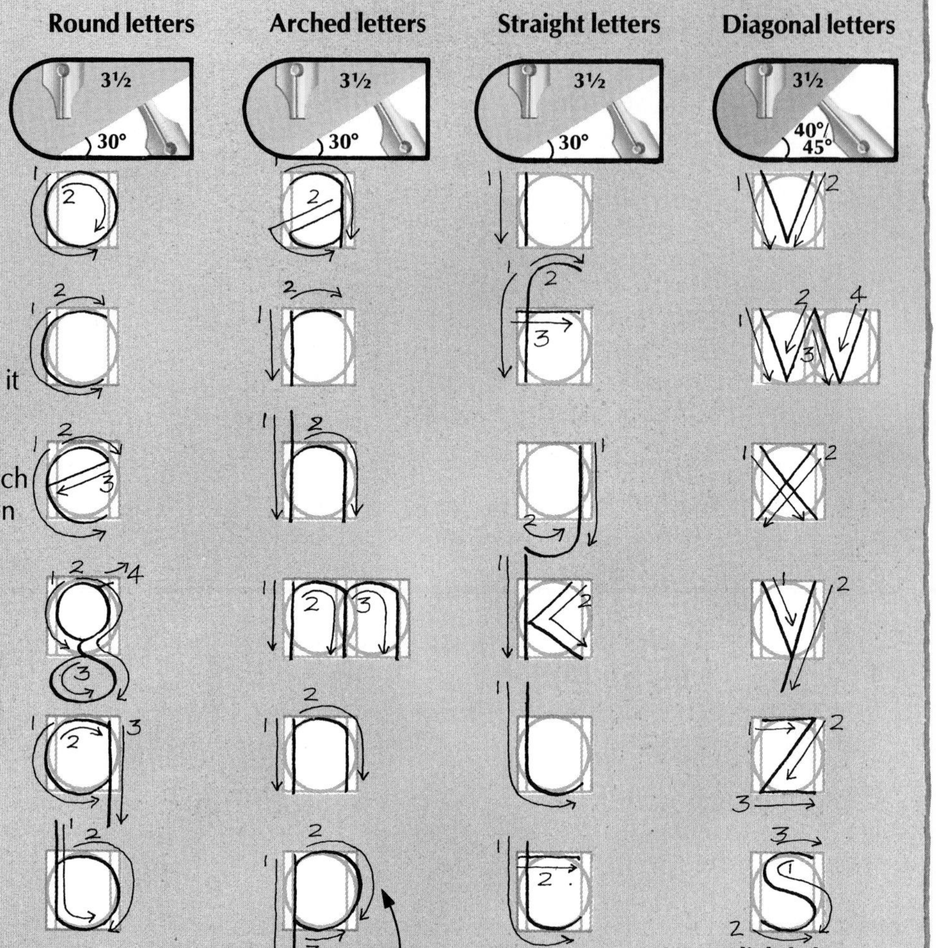

Round letters
Arched letters
Straight letters
Diagonal letters
3½
30°
40°/45°

The letter 'p' fits well in both Round and Arched groups.

Use a slightly less steep pen angle for strokes 2 and 3 of 's' and the center stroke of 'z'.

Writing skeletons

1. Fit a 3½ nib into your calligraphy pen and load it with ink.
2. Put tracing paper over each grid in turn, hold your pen at the correct angle and write the letters.

Breaking out

The main part, or body, of a minuscule is about 3/5 as high as a majuscule. The strokes that break out of the grid are called ascenders and descenders.

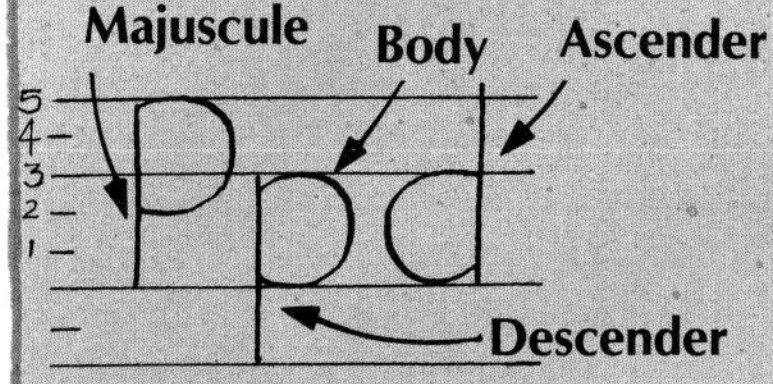

Majuscule
Body
Ascender
Descender

Basic shape

All Gothic letters (see page 16) have straight sides, like this 'o'.

All minuscules in one calligraphy style usually relate to the letter 'o'. It is called the basic shape. It is shown each time you learn a new style in this book.

x-height

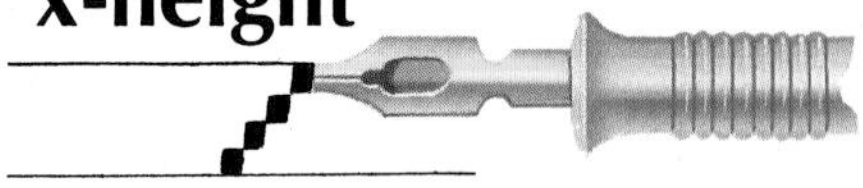

The height of the body of a minuscule is called its x-height. It is calculated in nib widths, made by holding your nib like this and making a short mark.

How high?

This x-height is 4 nib widths.

A picture like this shows you how high to make all the minuscules in this book. Ascenders and descenders are about ½ as long as the x-height.

Ruling up

If you are writing minuscules in calligraphy, you need to draw pencil guidelines their x-height apart. This is called ruling up.

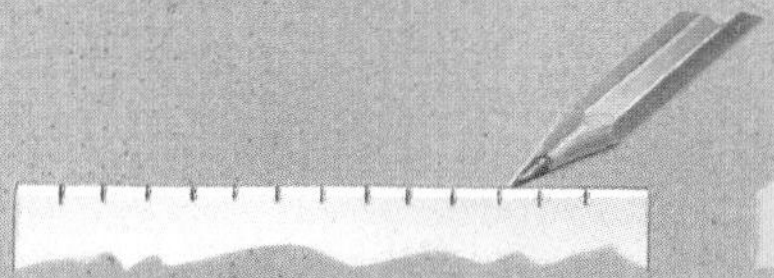

1

Use your set square and ruler to draw a straight line across your paper, as shown at the top of page 9.

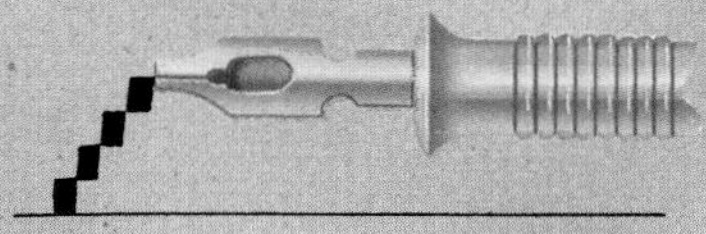

2

Make the right number of nib widths for the x-height on the left-hand margin. See how to do this on page 10.

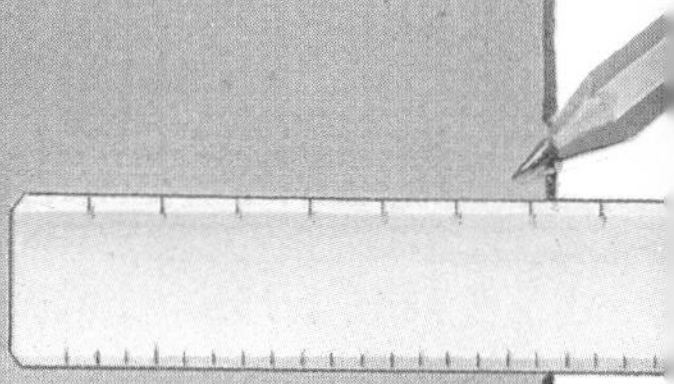

3

Rule a second line at the top of the x-height. Use your set square to start it if you need to.

The Foundational alphabet

This style, called Foundational, is closely based on the skeleton minuscules on page 9.

Below are the x-height and basic shape. Rule up, then try to copy the letters. Use the same pen angles as for the skeletons.

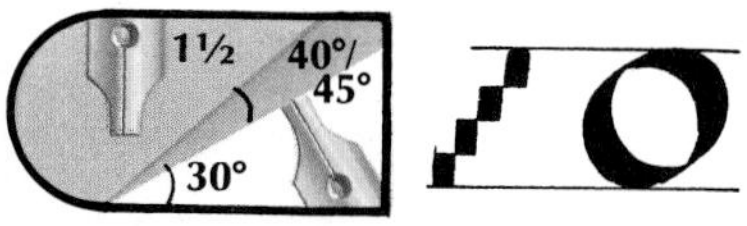

1½
40°
45°
30°

abcdefghi
jklmnopq
rstuvwxyz

Checkpoints

on

- Stand back from your letters. Check that the spaces inside the round and arched letters look the same size.

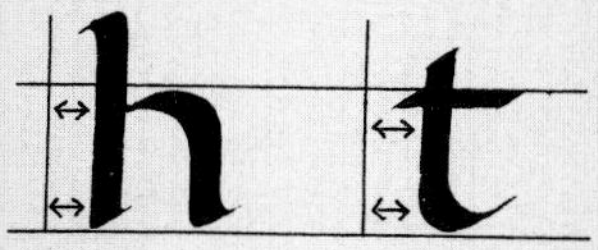

h t

- Check that your letters do not slope backwards. Use your set square to draw some straight vertical pencil lines through your writing line to guide you.

A calligraphy bookmark

Foundational letters are quite clear and simple, so they are useful for all sorts of purposes.

Try writing out a favorite saying or poem in Foundational letters. You could write it on a strip of colored cardboard to make a bookmark, like the one shown here.

You can use the capitals on page 9 with Foundational letters. Make them 6 nib widths high.

Leave the width of a small 'o' between words.

Leave twice the x-height between lines of writing, as shown here.

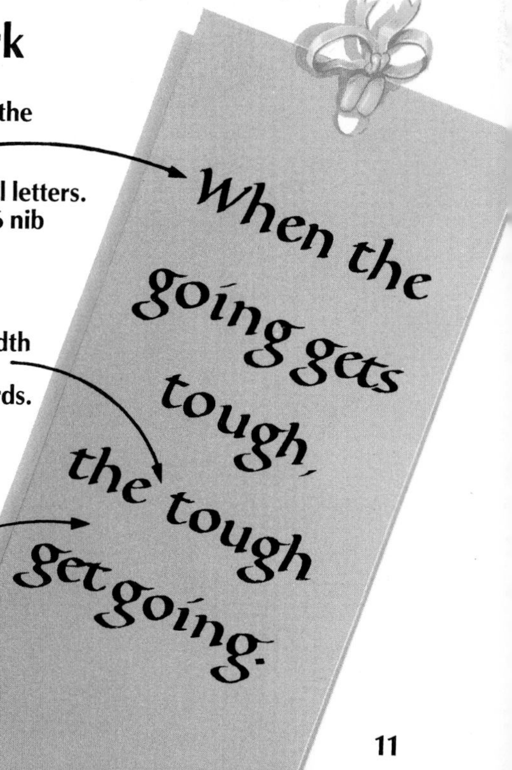

When the
going gets
tough,
the tough
get going.

The Look of Letters

The style and size of any calligraphy letters you write will make a powerful impression on your reader. Once you know a variety of styles, you can decide which one is best for each piece of work. The calligraphy letters shown on this page, called Uncials, are ideal for trying out different effects.

Uncials

Uncials were used from the 4th century forward. Although some Uncials had ascenders and descenders, they were not proper minuscules. These developed later.

Rule up a piece of paper using the x-height shown below. Then carefully copy the Uncial alphabet, following the arrows. Keep practicing until your letters look like those on the right.

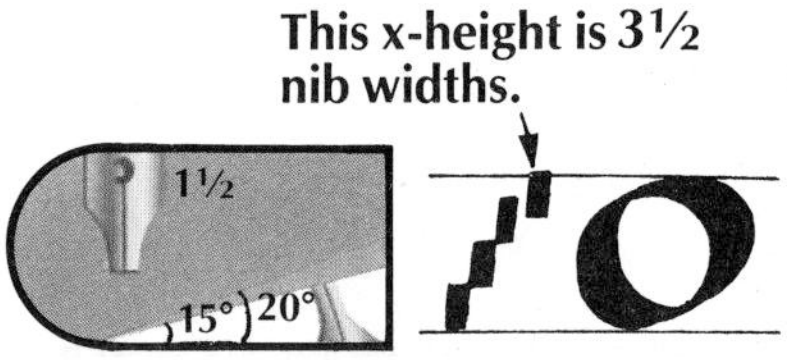

This x-height is 3½ nib widths.
1½
15°
20°

Use a 20° pen angle to write 'v','w','x' and 'y'.

Family tree

Uncials have a historical 'feel', so you could use them to write out your family tree. Try starting with yourself and working back through your family as far as you can. First, find out who married whom and if they had children. There are numbers on page 46 you could use for dates.

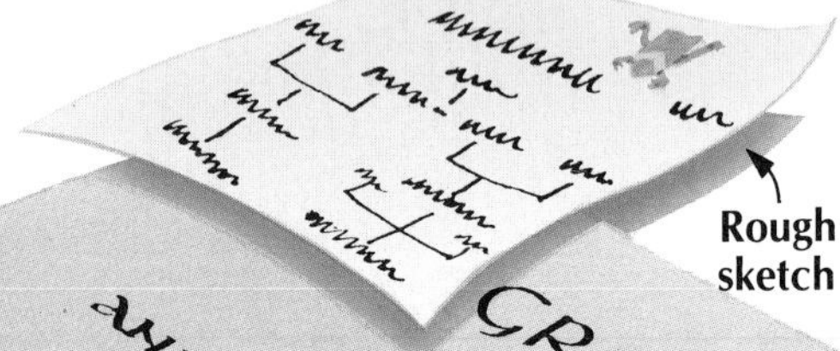

Rough sketch

1 Make a small rough sketch of your family tree. This will show you how much space it takes up on the page.

2 Draw the lines or 'branches' of your tree on your writing paper. Rule up writing guidelines where you will need to fill in names.

3 Write your family's names in Uncials. Write larger letters for capitals.

4 Go over the lines of the tree using a ruler and a felt-tip pen so that they are clear and crisp.

5 Erase your writing guidelines carefully.

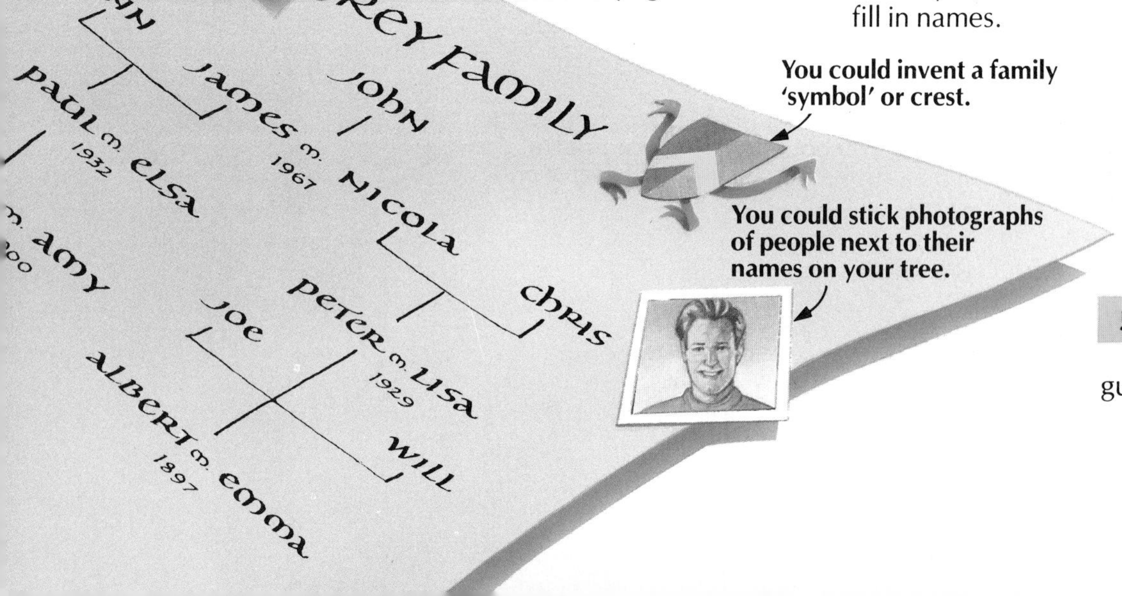

GREY FAMILY
ANN
JAMES m. 1967 NICOLA
JOHN
PAUL m. 1932 ELSA
m. AMY
PETER m. 1929 LISA
CHRIS
JOE
WILL
ALBERT m. 1897 EMMA
You could invent a family 'symbol' or crest.
You could stick photographs of people next to their names on your tree.

Letter weight

You can alter the impression a letter makes in two simple ways. You can write it with a different nib, or change its x-height. This affects what is called the letter's 'weight', (how dark or light it looks). There are examples of different weights of calligraphy letters below.

Changing the nib

alphabet

alphabet

These words are the same x-height but they were written with different nibs. The second word, written with a thicker nib, looks darker and is longer.

Changing the x-height

alphabet

alphabet

These words were written with the same nib, but have different x-heights. The first word looks much denser or heavier and takes up less space.

Tip

Try out a selection of nibs and letter heights when you are planning a piece of calligraphy.

heavy writing is dark, clear and strong

LIGHTWEIGHT WRITING MAKES A PATTERN OF STROKES

Writing an invitation

You could try out the effects of different weights of calligraphy letters by writing an invitation to a party.

1 Make a list of the information your invitation must have on it. (What is happening, where and when.)

Try decorating your invitations with pictures that go with the mood of the party.

2 Decide which words are most important. What do you want to catch the reader's eye first? Which must be biggest?

3 The lettering style can give an impression of what the party will be like. Try out different styles, sizes and weights on scratch paper.

4 When you are happy with the look of the letters, rule up your paper and write out your invitation.

LOOKING AT LAYOUT

The way pictures and writing (text) are arranged on the page is called layout. It is just as important as the lettering style you choose and gives your work its impact. The ideas here will help you decide the best layout for each piece of calligraphy.

Basic layouts

These pictures show five basic ways of laying out your calligraphy. There are many more you can try for yourself.

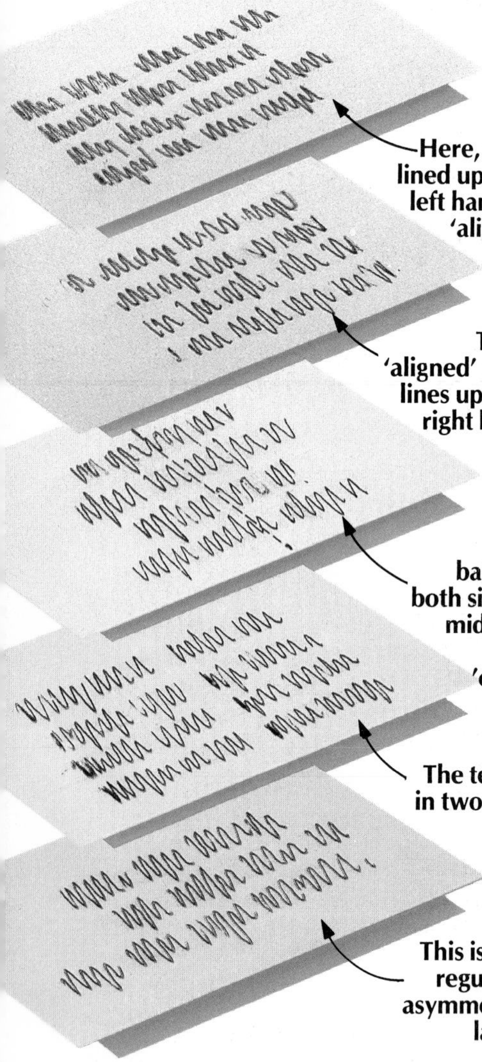

Here, the text is lined up along the left hand side, or 'aligned' left.

This text is 'aligned' right, as it lines up along the right hand side.

Here, the writing is balanced on both sides of the middle of the page, or 'centered'.

The text here is in two columns.

This is a less regular, or asymmetrical layout.

You may find it tricky to choose the best layout for some pieces. Try out as many ideas as you can. In the end, your choice will often be a matter of personal taste.

Unusual layouts

Sometimes you may feel that the overall impact of a piece of calligraphy is more important than being able to read the words easily.

Here are some examples of more unusual layouts. If you want to try some yourself, draw some pencil guidelines of the shape you want before you start writing.

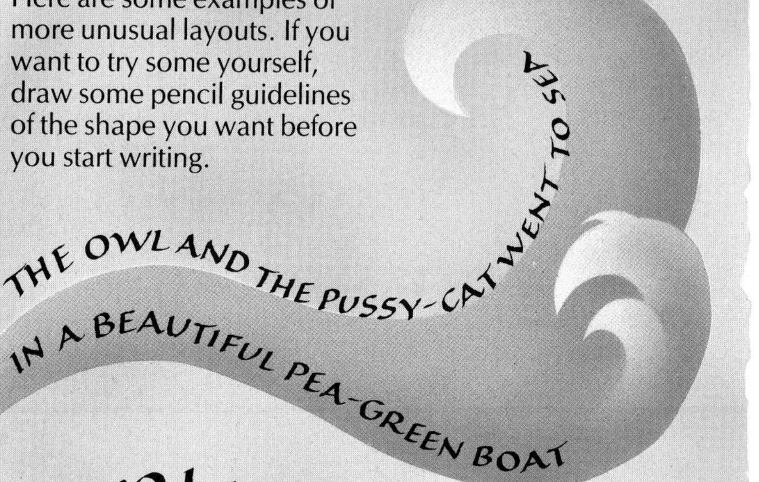
THE OWL AND THE PUSSY-CAT WENT TO SEA
IN A BEAUTIFUL PEA-GREEN BOAT

This layout follows the shape of a wave to create the right mood for this piece.

we · wish · you · a · merry · christmas · and · a · happy · new · year ·

Start writing in the middle and turn the paper as you write for this layout.

THIS WAY

These letters have been slightly 'stretched' to fit this layout.

Cut and paste

Here is one way of trying out several possible layouts before writing your final piece. It is called cut and paste.

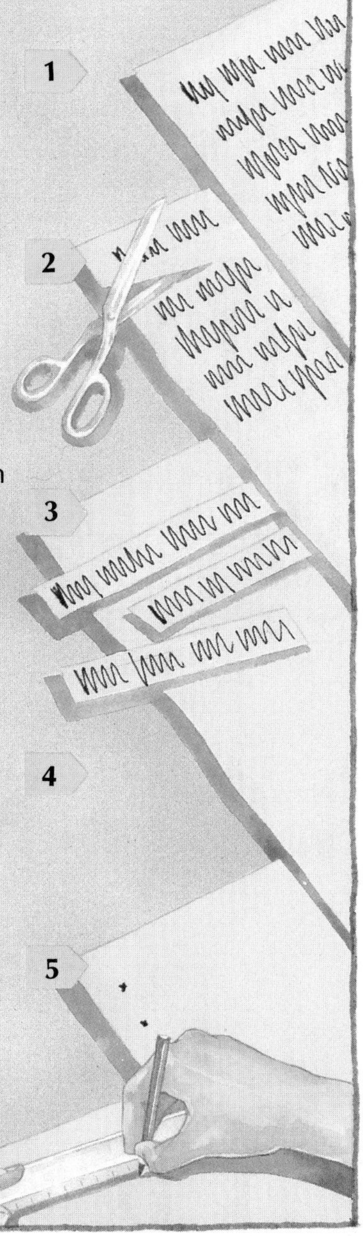

1 Write your calligraphy piece out quite carefully. Use a piece of scratch paper as this is not the finished work.

2 Cut the text into strips of paper, with a line of writing on each strip.

3 Put the strips on top of another sheet of scratch paper. Move them around until you are happy with the way they are arranged.

4 Stick them down with rubber cement. (You can move the strips if you want to with this glue.)

5 Measuring from the top and the sides of the paper, mark where each line begins. Make marks in the same places on your writing paper and rule up.

Choosing margins

The areas of blank page around your calligraphy are called margins. Their size can give your work a spacious, airy feel or a dark, dense look. Here's a simple way of choosing them.

1 It's a good idea to work on a bigger piece of paper than you really need. You can always trim it, but you cannot add anything back on.

2 Cut four long strips of colored cardboard or stiff paper. Stick them together in pairs to make two right angled corners.

3 Lay the two right angles of cardboard around your work. Keep moving them until you are happy with the margin space you can see.

4 Make small pencil marks in each corner to show where you will trim. Remove the cardboard and trim your paper using a ruler and a craft knife or scalpel.

Margin hints

The method of choosing margins above will soon help you judge them by eye. Some pieces can cause problems, however. Here are some tips on solving them.

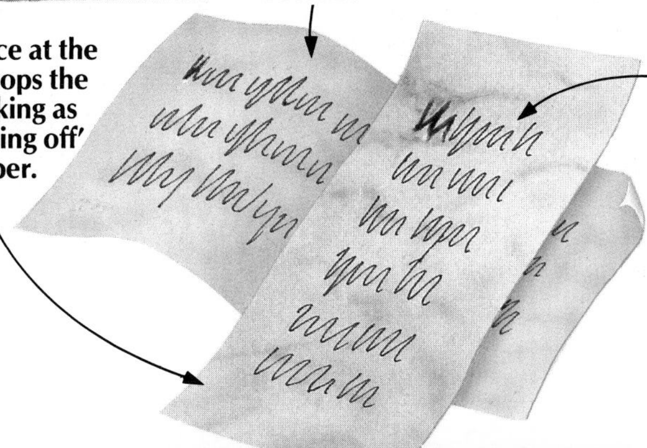

A short, wide piece needs more space at the sides than at the top and the bottom.

Extra space at the bottom stops the piece looking as if it is 'falling off' of the paper.

Tall, thin work needs less space at the sides and more at the top and bottom.

Gothic Letters

Gothic is one of the most popular calligraphy styles. It is often called Black Letter because of the strong, dark impression the letters make. Gothic makes a dramatic impact on the page, but it is not the best style to use for work that needs to be easy to read as the letters are quite complicated.

Gothic minuscules

All Gothic minuscules are formed from straight strokes, even those that are curved or round in other styles. Ascenders and descenders are short.

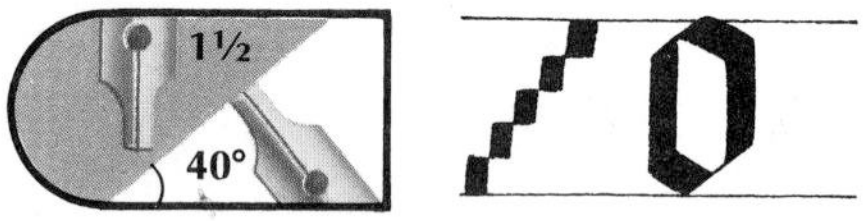

Rule up some paper and copy all the letters, following the numbered strokes and arrows.

Gothic capitals

Gothic capitals are quite tricky to learn. These are a reasonably simple version*. Try writing each letter on tracing paper laid over this page first. When you feel ready, rule up and copy each letter on to paper.

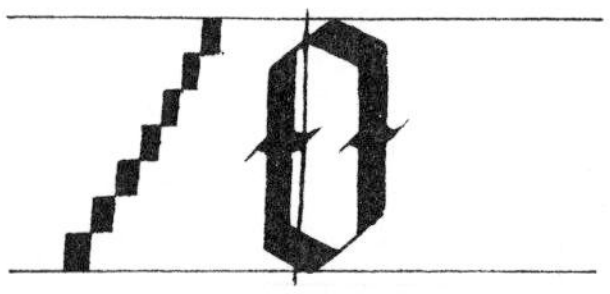

Turn your nib to make this stroke as thin as possible.

Checkpoint

- Put paper over the top and bottom of some letters. You should see lots of straight strokes, as shown here.

*You can find a more complicated Gothic alphabet on page 40.

Writing a certificate

Gothic letters look quite impressive, so they are ideal for official-looking pieces of work.

You could write a certificate using Gothic lettering. It could be a serious award, or a joke, like the one shown here.

1. Decide what words you want on your certificate and what size and weight they should be (see page 13).
2. Write out the words on scratch paper and then choose your layout using cut and paste (see page 15). Rule up a piece of paper ready to write.
3. Load your pen and write the words on your certificate in Gothic letters.

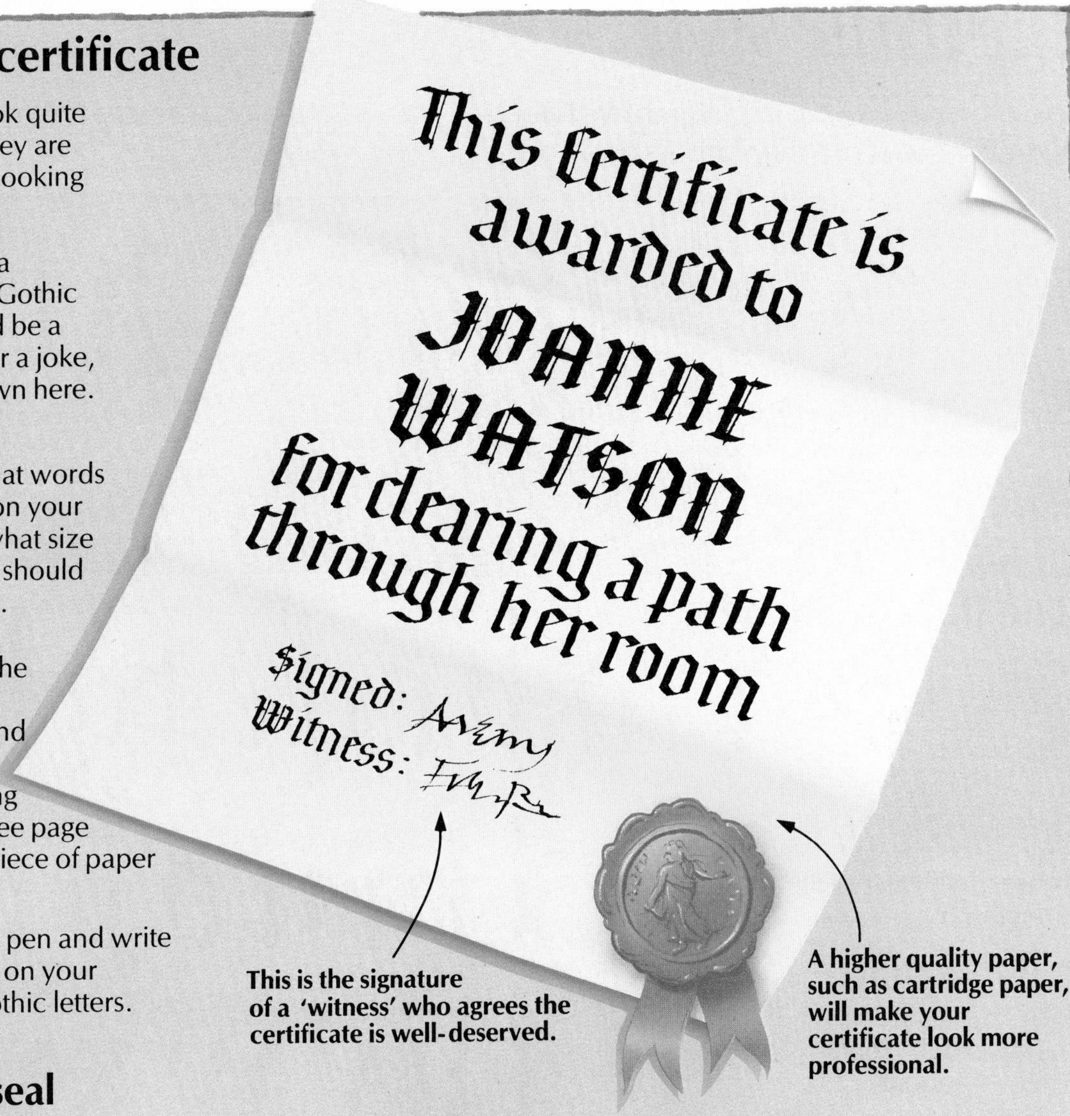
This Certificate is awarded to
JOANNE WATSON
for clearing a path through her room
Signed:
Witness:

This is the signature of a 'witness' who agrees the certificate is well-deserved.

A higher quality paper, such as cartridge paper, will make your certificate look more professional.

Making a seal

Old documents often had a wax seal at the bottom. Here's how to make one using two strips of ribbon and a candle.

1. Lay the ribbons on your certificate. Light the candle and let wax drip onto one end of both strips.
2. Wait for the wax to cool slightly. Then press a coin into it. Take the coin off straight up and leave your seal to dry.

Medieval letter

To practice the Gothic style, try writing a 'medieval' letter to a friend. You could use old-fashioned words like 'ye' instead of 'the' and 'thou' instead of 'you'.

Gothic projects

Gothic writing can be used to give a dramatic effect. See pages 52, 73 and 75 for a variety of projects using gothic calligraphy.

DRACULA
Wurst
AC/DC

The Italic Style

Italic is a very popular calligraphy style. It is quicker to write than others and you can adapt it into an elegant handwriting style to use every day, too.

Italic facts

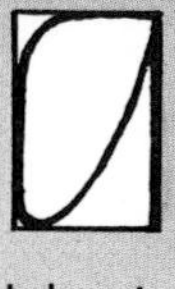

1 The grid that Italic letters are based on is an oval inside a rectangle. The basic shape is an 'a' not an 'o'.

2 The way some Italic letters are written creates small triangles of space between some strokes, like those above.

3 Italic letters lean slightly to the right. Look at the 5° slope of these letters to help you judge how far they should lean.

The Italic alphabet

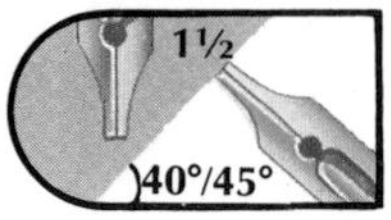

In the Italic alphabet, many pen strokes have built-in 'hook' serifs. These help you start the strokes. Write each letter as smoothly as you can.

Italic capitals

Italic capitals are slightly narrower than Roman capitals. They lean about 5° to the right as well. You can find a whole alphabet to copy on page 41.

Added extras

During the Renaissance*, when people first used Italics, they often added decorative strokes to the letters. Some examples are shown below.

If you want to use them, be careful that your work doesn't get too cluttered.

Some writers added loops to their ascenders and descenders.

Some Italic capitals had extra strokes called swashes. They were added to the end of pen strokes.

Queen Elizabeth 1 of England used a highly decorative Italic style. She added strokes called flourishes to her signature in 1570.

**This was a time of great artistic activity in Europe, during the 15th and 16th centuries.*

Writing a notice

Italics are often used for menus or notices because they are attractive and easy to read. Writing a notice to pin up on a board is a good way to develop a smooth style.

1. Think about what size lettering to use for each piece of information on your notice. Some may be more important than others.
2. Write the words out on scratch paper. Choose the best layout with cut and paste, as shown on page 15.
3. Now write your notice out properly. Try to build up a rhythm of even, sloping pen strokes.
4. When you have finished, pin your work up and stand back to check that the lettering is smooth and clear.

You could cut your notice into an eye-catching shape, like these.

Fly your kite with us
ainting classes
Every Monday at the Art Centre 7-9 pm
FOR SALE
Fender Stratocaster
ellent condition
See Paul Smith

Italic handwriting

For everyday handwriting, try writing Italic letters in one continuous stroke. You will also find it quicker to join some letters together. Here are some of the main ways letters are linked. There is a complete handwriting alphabet on page 42.

1. Extend the 'hook' at the end of a letter up to the top of the next letter.
2. Join some letters together with horizontal strokes like those on the left.
3. Some letters, such as 'b', 'p' and 's', look better if only joined together on the left.

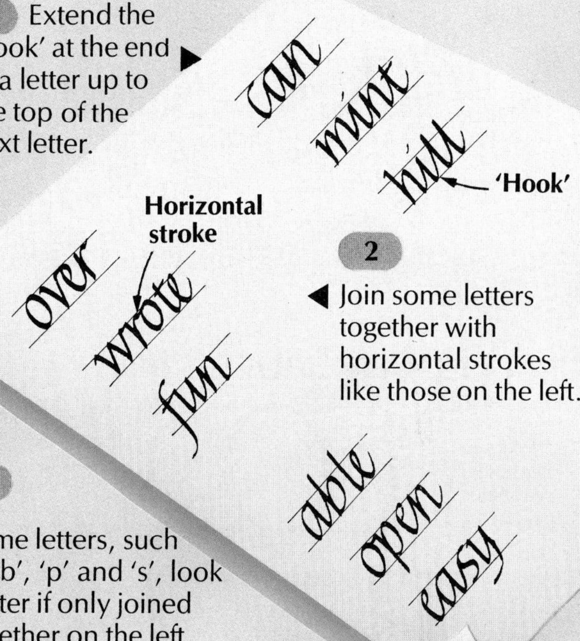

can
mint
hill
'Hook'
Horizontal stroke
over
wrote
fun
able
open
easy

With practice, you will find you join letters naturally as your own writing style develops.

Using Italic handwriting

Italic lettering is suitable for all kinds of objects. Try using it on a folder or 'presenter' for a school project. There are a variety of projects in the second part of this book which use Italic lettering. You could use an Italic felt-tip or fountain pen instead of a dip pen for the projects. These are available at most stationer's.

You could stick your souvenirs at different angles, as shown here, to add interest.

steam train tickets
TUESDAY
The view from the train
The pony near the station
Our route

BUILT-UP LETTERS

The letters below are called Versals. They were often used to start a verse or chapter in medieval books. Each part of a Versal is built up with several pen strokes. The outline strokes are made first and then filled in with a central stroke.

Versal facts

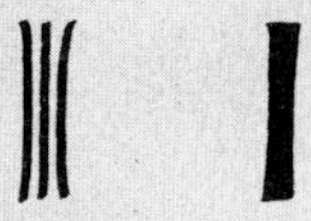

Nib making main stroke.
Nib turned around to make a serif.

In the first picture, the strokes of a Versal 'O' are separated. You write them touching each other to make the finished letter.

Some parts of Versal letters are narrower in the middle. You need to make their two outside strokes curve in slightly, as shown above.

To write the main strokes of Versals, turn your pen to make them as wide as possible. For serifs, turn your nib to make them as thin as you can.

The Versal alphabet

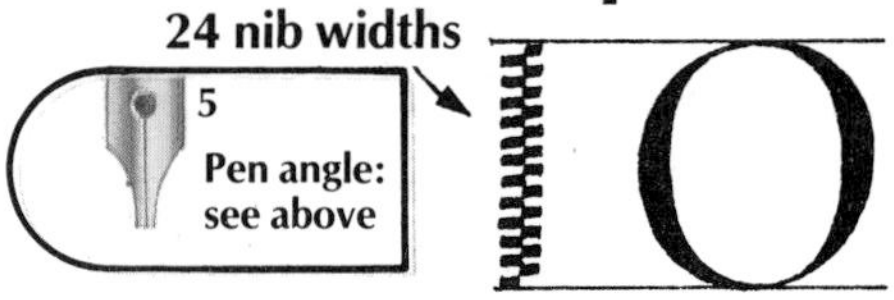
24 nib widths
5
Pen angle: see above

These Versals are not filled in, to show you how they are formed. You can fill them in using the finished Versals on page 41 to check your letters.

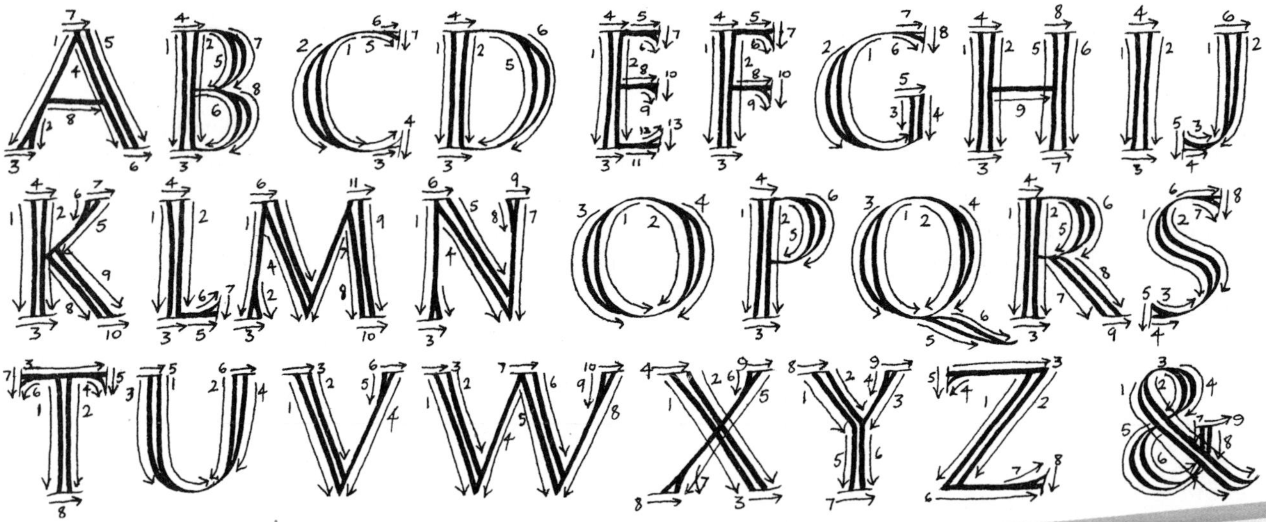

Versatile Versals

Versals are useful for all sorts of pieces. Here are some less traditional ways of using them.

Here, Versals are written at different heights.

These are 'open' Versals, without the center stroke filled in.

ROMEO & JULIET
PARIS

Painted letters

Large Versals were often painted gold or rich colors in early manuscripts.*

Here's how to fill in the outline of a Versal letter with colored paint. You can adapt this method for other styles of lettering, too.

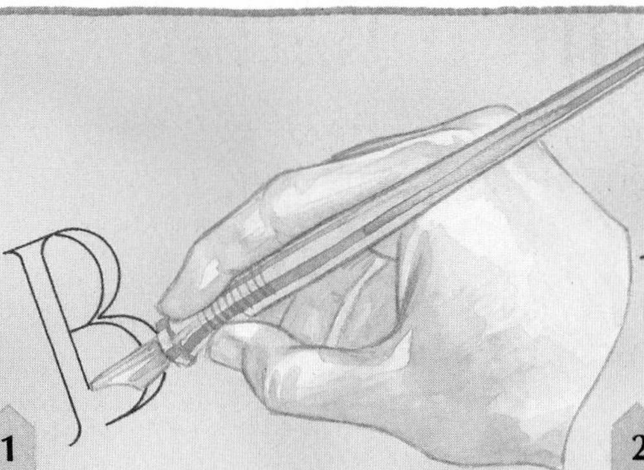

1 Make the outer strokes of the letter with your calligraphy pen, using a thin nib, such as a 5.

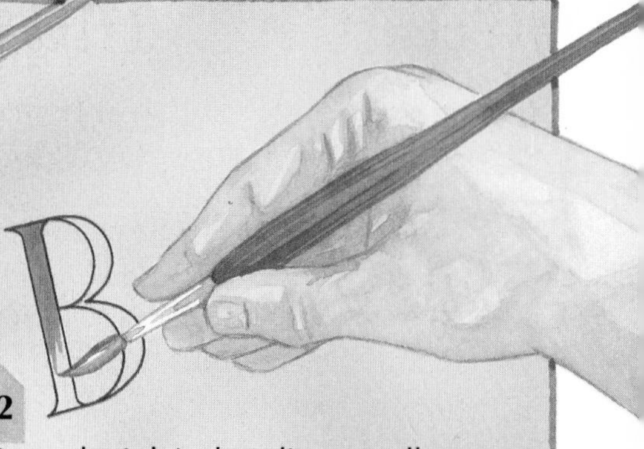

2 Once the ink is dry, dip a small brush in watercolor or gouache paint and fill in the letter.

Patterned letters

Write some large letters with wide pens like those on page 5. Trace around their outlines and fill them in with patterns to produce letters like these.

Message on a T-shirt

You can use fabric paints to write on material. Here is one method of painting on a T-shirt. A different technique can be found on pages 74-75.

You will need:

A clean, plain T-shirt (a cotton one is best).

Tracing paper.

A hard and a soft pencil.

A small, pointed paintbrush.

Fabric paint from a craft shop (follow the manufacturer's instructions for setting it).

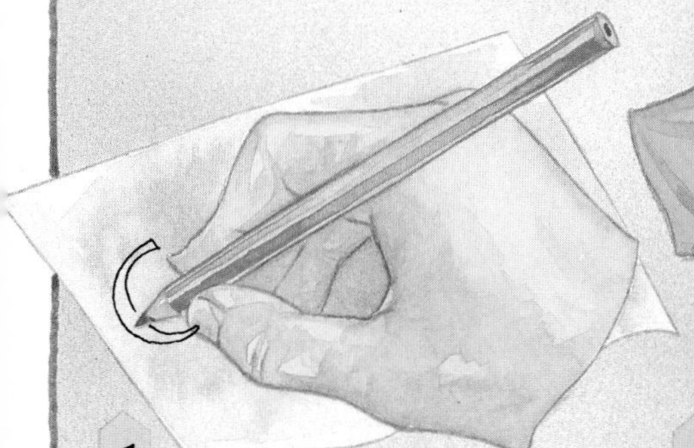

1 Draw the letters onto some tracing-paper with a hard pencil. Turn the sheet over and scribble hard over the back of the letters with a soft pencil.

2 Tape the sheet face up on the T-shirt in the right position. Go over the letters with a hard pencil to transfer them onto the shirt.

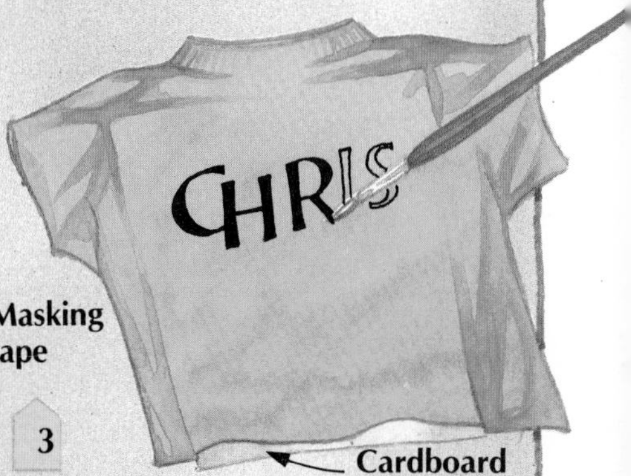

3 Put a sheet of cardboard inside the T-shirt. Paint the outline of each letter first and then carefully fill it in with paint using your small paintbrush.

*See page 23 for more about decorating letters.

Decoration and Illumination

Calligraphers throughout history have decorated their work. Your decoration can be quite simple and still look effective, as these ideas show.

Beautiful borders

A patterned border makes an attractive frame for calligraphy. Don't make it too wide, or it will overpower your lettering. Here are some ideas to try.

There are more border patterns on pages 45 and 67.

Load some ink into your calligraphy pen and make a pattern of pen strokes around the edge of your writing paper.

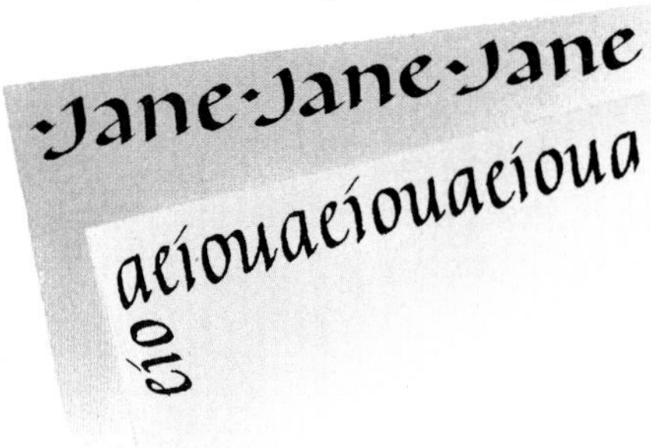

Try writing the alphabet you are using, your name, or the title of the piece in a border around your work.

Move the stencil around the edges.

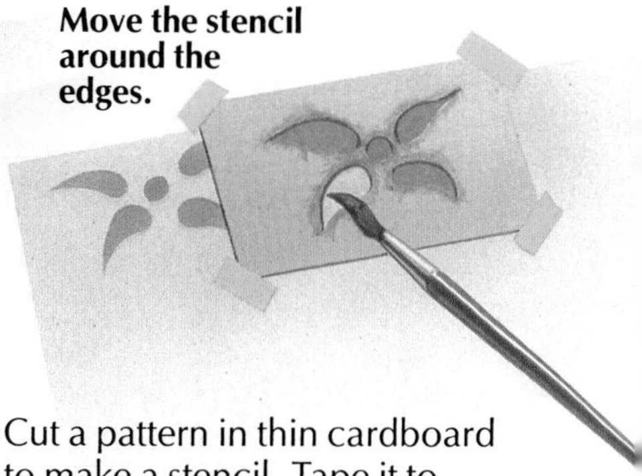

Cut a pattern in thin cardboard to make a stencil. Tape it to each edge of your work in turn. Add color through the holes.*

Pen pictures

You can draw pictures with your pen to decorate your calligraphy.

1 Draw or trace a picture or cartoon onto your paper with a fairly hard pencil.

2 Draw over the pencil lines with your calligraphy pen, using a medium or narrow nib.

This shading is made with criss cross pen strokes. It is called cross-hatching.

Design a name plate

You could combine lettering and decoration by designing a name plate on thin cardboard for your bedroom door. The designs shown here will give you some ideas for choosing decoration that matches your lettering style.

A border of straight pen strokes goes well with dark Gothic letters.

Delicate drawings look best with Italics.

These Roman capitals go well with geometric shapes.

For more about stencils see pages 34 and 70.

Illumination

In the Middle Ages, capital letters were often richly decorated, like the one on the left. Adding the gold and then color decoration was called illuminating the letter. You can find out how to do it below.

The text was arranged around an illuminated capital as shown here.

Gilding

In illumination, the gold is applied before any color. This is called gilding.

Real gold leaf is very expensive. The method shown here uses thin sheets of gold called transfer gold which is inexpensive. Good art shops sell it.

You will need:

An equal amount of household glue and water mixed together, with a little gouache paint* added to it.

A sheet of transfer gold.

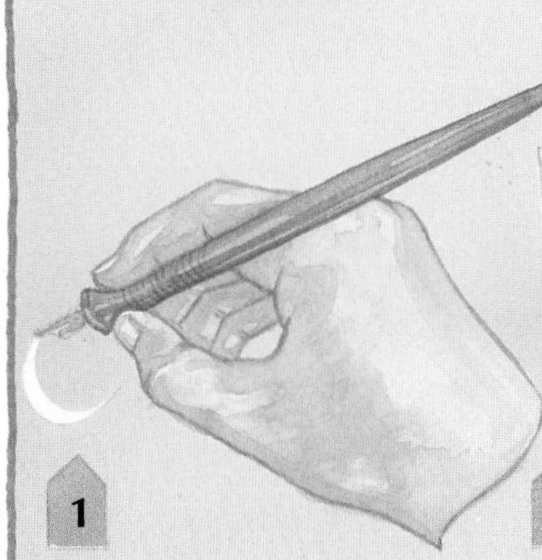

1 Load a mixture of glue, water and a little gouache into your pen. Write the letter outline, then carefully fill it in.

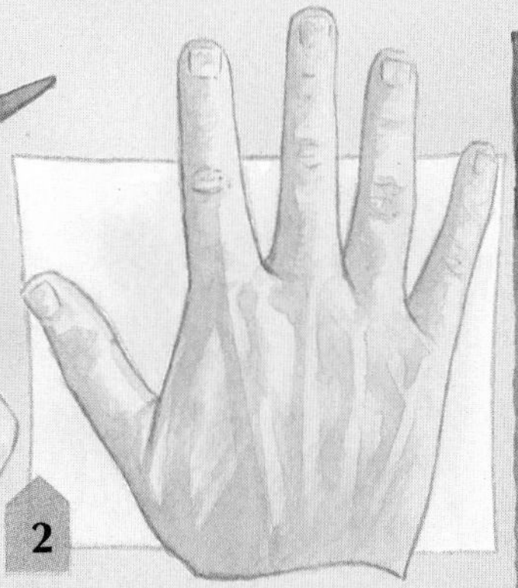

2 After about 30 minutes, breathe on the letter to make it sticky again. Put the transfer gold over it and press down firmly.

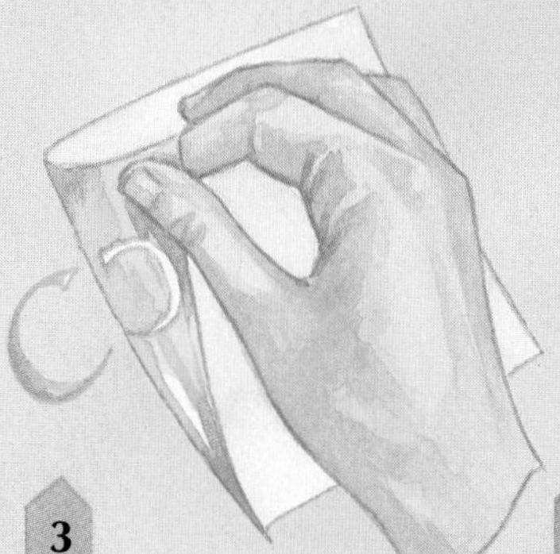

3 Take the sheet off. If gold has not stuck to the whole letter, repeat step 2 until it is covered.

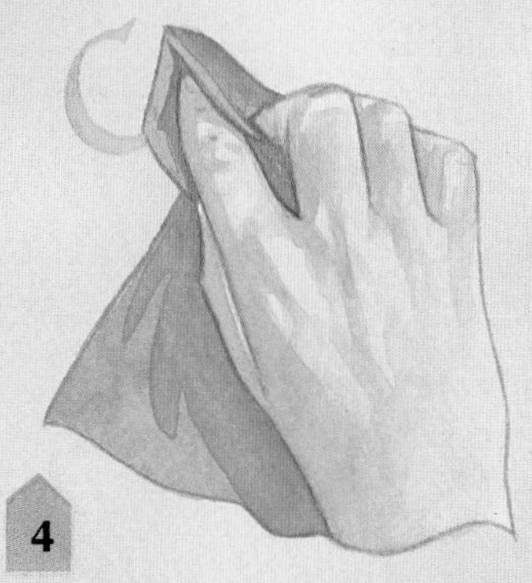

4 Rub your gold letter carefully with a soft piece of cloth to make it shine. This is called burnishing.

Decoration

Add decoration around your gilded letter that suits the purpose of the piece. Here are some examples.

You could add sparkles to a letter.

Try decorating your letter with flowers.

Illuminate a letter with simple pictures.

This illuminated capital is based on a traditional design.

Cheap gold

Here are some more cheap materials which will also color your work gold.

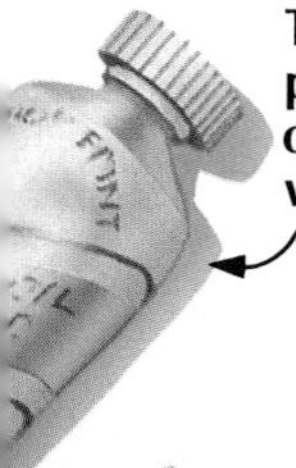

This gold gouache paint can be used on its own or mixed with water.

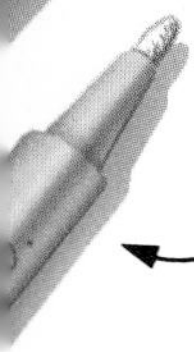

Gold felt-tip pens are good for outlines but the ink can develop a dark outline, or 'halo' on the page.

This gold-colored powder can be mixed with gum arabic (from art shops) and water, then loaded into a pen.

*You can find out more about gouache paint on page 32.

Cards and Presents

You can use your calligraphy skills to make original cards and presents.

Paper and cardboard

You can make cards out of many different sorts of paper or cardboard. Below are the main types of paper and cardboard available, with tips on when to use them.

Layout paper is ideal for scratch paper and for some finished work.

Cartridge paper gives a 'classier' look to cards, certificates and posters.

Ingres and Caslon papers are easy to write on and look good.

Handmade paper is expensive, but is ideal for special pieces of work.

Textured paper produces interesting lettering effects.

Art shops stock thin cardboard in many thicknesses and colors.

Making cards

There are lots of different ways to fold paper to make a card. Use a craft knife to score the folds neatly (see page 79). There are some more ideas for cards and envelopes on pages 54-55.

This card was folded in half diagonally and then in half again.

A concertina card

Here's a card which is ideal for writing a joke or a rhyme inside.

You will need:

A sheet of cardboard about 10cm x 30cm.

40cm of ribbon.

A hole punch.

If your card has six sections, each one is 5 cm wide.

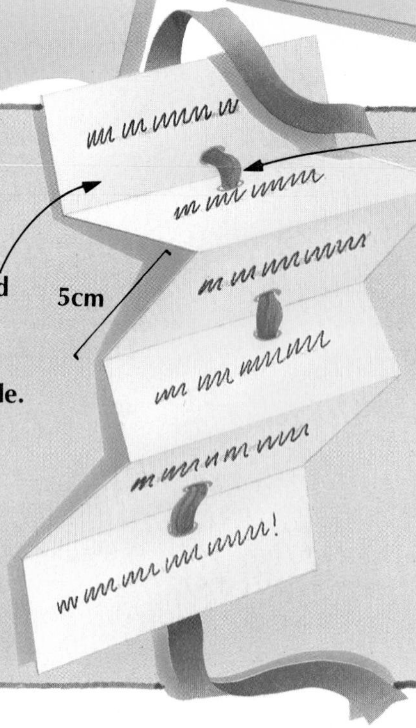

1 Work out the number of lines in your joke or rhyme. Fold the card backwards and forwards into equal sections like a concertina.

2 Rule up and write one line on each section, starting at the top.

3 Mark the middle of each alternate fold, starting at the top. Punch a hole through each mark.

4 With the card still folded, thread the ribbon through the holes and tie the ends in a bow.

Writing on glass

You can even paint some calligraphy on a glass. Here's how to do it.

1 To work out how big your letters should be, write them in several sizes on some paper and hold them against the glass.

MARIA

2 Tape the paper 'pattern' you choose to the inside of the glass where you want the letters to be.

MAR
Ease the paper up against the curved part of the glass.

3 Using a small paintbrush and glass paint from a craft shop, carefully paint in the letters.

MAR

Wipe mistakes off while the paint is still wet, using a rag dipped in turpentine or white spirit*.

4 When the paint is dry, take the pattern out. Wash the glass out thoroughly with hot soapy water.

MARIA

You can find out how to make calligraphy giftwrap and tags on pages 34, 35 and 58-59.

Framing your calligraphy

Framed calligraphy looks more professional. Here's how to make a simple frame.

1 Leave 3cm extra paper outside your margins (see page 15). Cut two pieces of cardboard or mounting board* to the same size as your worksheet.

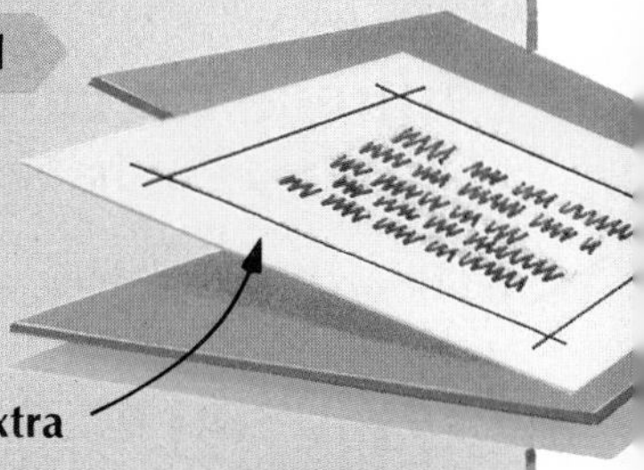
3 cm extra

2 Put spots of glue around the edge of a sheet of cardboard. Lay your worksheet on the cardboard, put some tracing paper over it and press down with your palm.

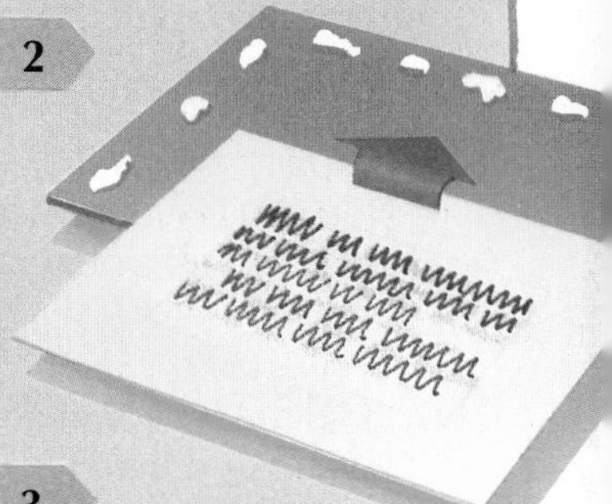

3 Measure and mark a 3cm strip around the second sheet of cardboard. Put your ruler against each line and cut the center out, leaving a frame.

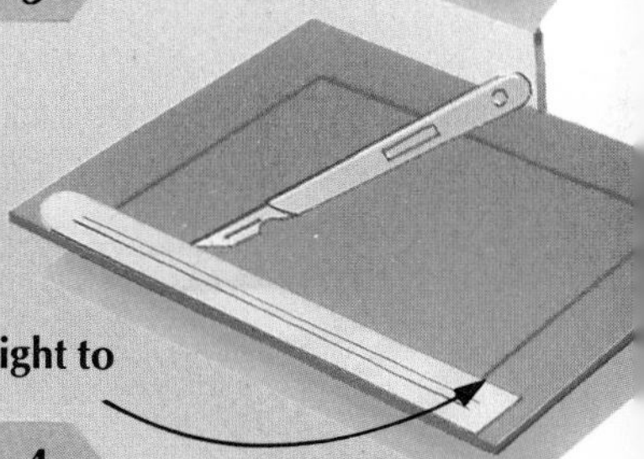
Don't cut right to the edge.

4 Put spots of glue around the edge of one side of the frame. Place it carefully over your worksheet so that the edges line up. Press down firmly.

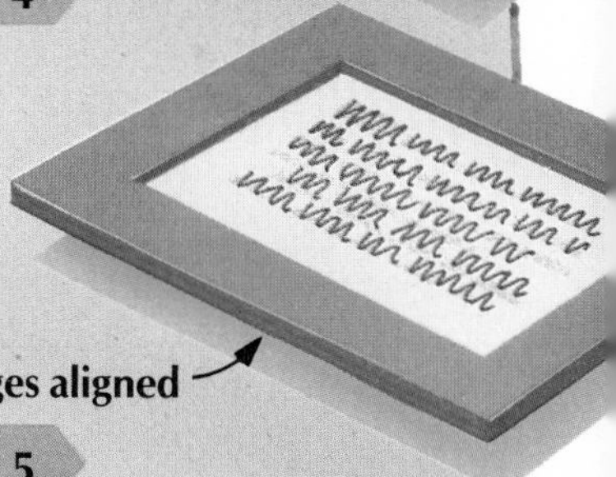
Edges aligned

5 Tape a loop of ribbon or a curtain ring onto the back sheet of cardboard if you want to hang your frame on the wall.

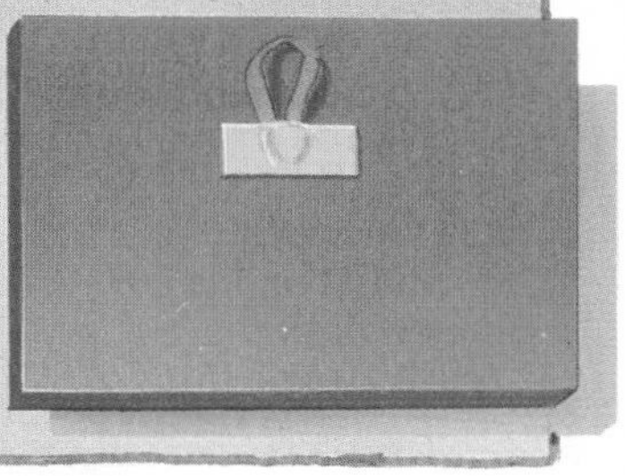

** You can buy these liquids from hardware shops but take great care when using them.*

**Mounting board is available from art shops.*

CHINESE CALLIGRAPHY

Chinese calligraphy looks uncluttered and spacious. It is traditionally written with a bamboo brush. You can use one to give your calligraphy an Oriental look, too.

Chinese brushes

Here are some of the brushes Chinese calligraphers use. You can get them at good art shops. A wide bamboo brush with bristles is the best one to start with.

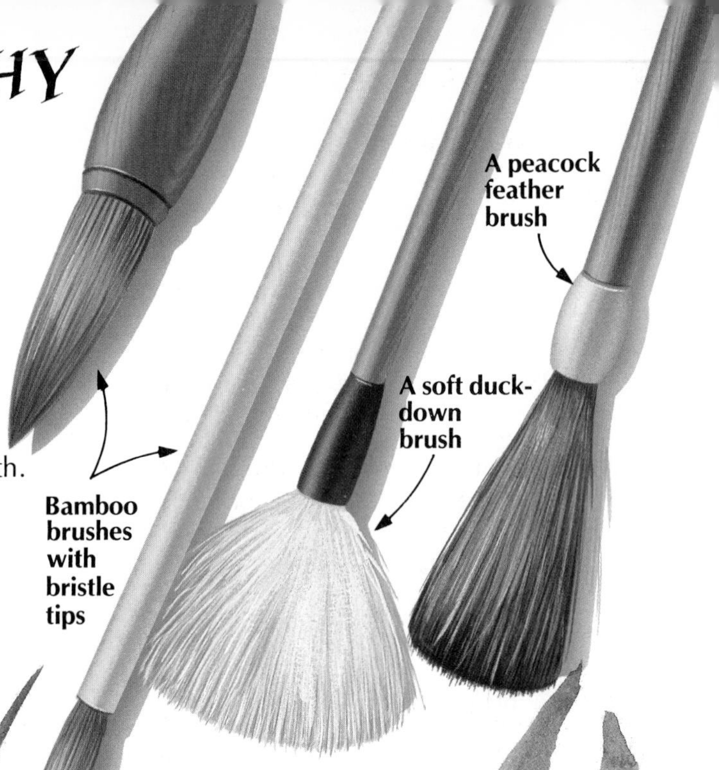

A peacock feather brush
A soft duck-down brush
Bamboo brushes with bristle tips

Preparing to write

You need to lay your drawing board flat for Oriental calligraphy. The different strokes are made by varying how hard you press your brush down.

1 Tape some scratch paper (newspaper is ideal) under your writing sheet. This will soak up moisture from your brush strokes.

2 Dip the whole brush in water and then the last ⅔ of the bristles at the tip, in ink.

3 Hold the brush upright, with your fingers arranged as shown in the picture below.

Start with light pressure on the tip, press down harder, then lift the brush up slowly for this stroke.
Flick the brush tip away from you to make these strokes.
Lay the whole brush down and then lift it up to get these short strokes.

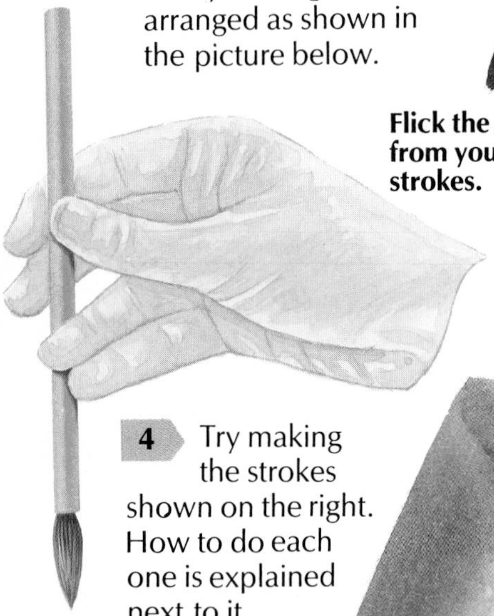

4 Try making the strokes shown on the right. How to do each one is explained next to it.

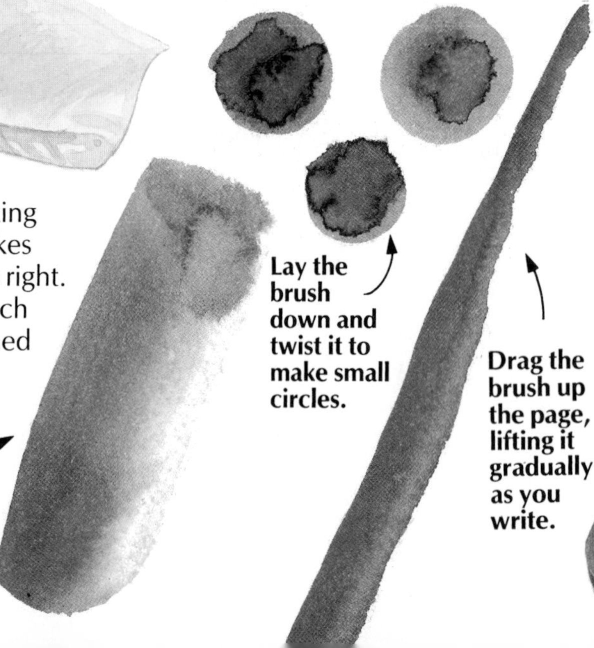

Lay the bristles down flat on the paper. Push the brush away from you.
Lay the brush down and twist it to make small circles.
Drag the brush up the page, lifting it gradually as you write.

Ink stones

Chinese calligraphers use ink made by grinding an ink stick with a little water in an ink stone. Some art shops sell them if you want to try it.

Ink stick
Ink stone

Writing a Chinese character

The Chinese alphabet is made up of characters. A character stands for an idea, not just one letter. Each character has several types of brush strokes.

There is not enough room to show the whole alphabet here, but this character contains the eight basic strokes of Chinese calligraphy. They are all made by varying the pressure you put on the brush, as shown on page 26.

Following the direction of the arrows with your brush, make each stroke of the character in the right order. Don't worry if you need to practice this several times before it looks right.

This character means 'eternity' in Chinese.

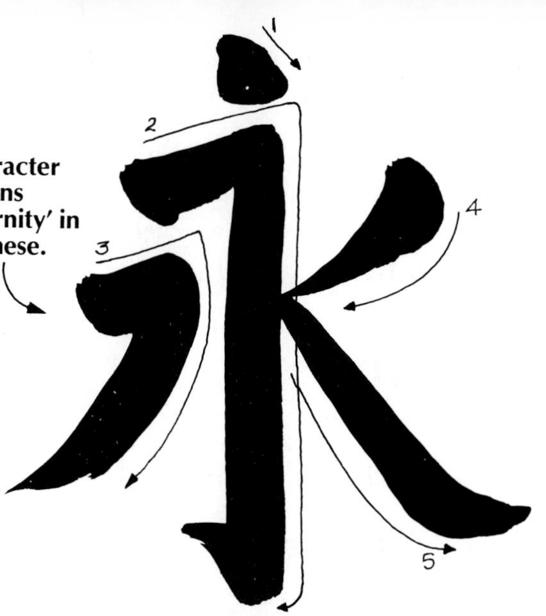
永
1
2
3
4
5

Making a Chinese scroll

Chinese characters are usually written one under the other, not across the page. The three characters below mean 'long life, good luck and happiness'. Try writing them on a long sheet of paper to look like an Oriental scroll.

To write the characters, follow the arrows below, in order, with your brush.

These pictures were made up of some of the brush strokes on the opposite page.

福
祿
壽

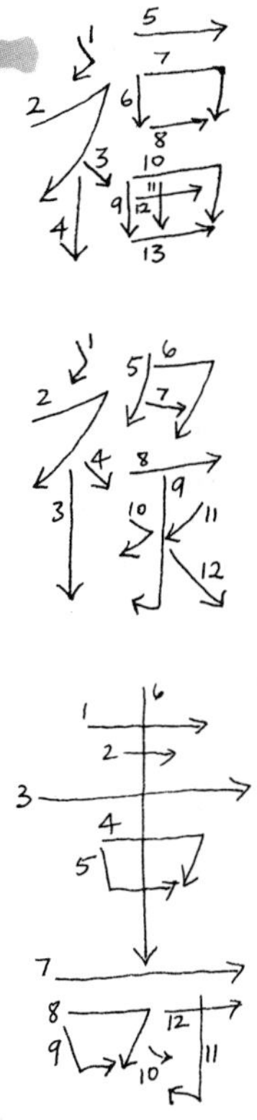

Brush pictures

You can easily give other calligraphy styles a spacious, Oriental 'feel'. You could write the words one under the other, or add brush stroke illustrations like the ones shown here.

Chinese brush paintings are usually of natural things, such as trees and flowers.

THIS BOOK BELONGS TO..
Once upon a time lived a
FOR MUM

DIFFERENT TOOLS

You don't always have to use a special type of pen to write calligraphy letters, as you saw on pages 26-27. Try out as many different types of writing tools as you can, or even make you own as shown on pages 4-5 and 58-59.

Calligraphy brushes

Art shops sell broad-edged calligraphy brushes like the ones below. They are not expensive and come in several sizes. Here you can see some of the effects they create. There is a complete brush alphabet to try on page 43.

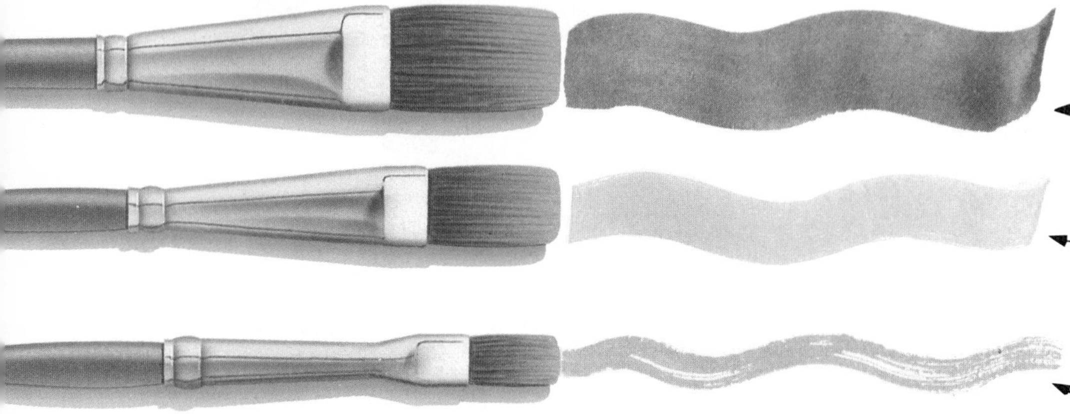

Wide brushes make very large, heavyweight strokes like these.

A medium brush was dipped in watered-down ink to create this effect.

A small brush was dipped in ink and then wiped with a tissue to make these strokes.

Automatic pens

The two pens below are called automatic pens. They have wide, split nibs and are useful for creating special effects or writing wide strokes. You can buy them from art shops.

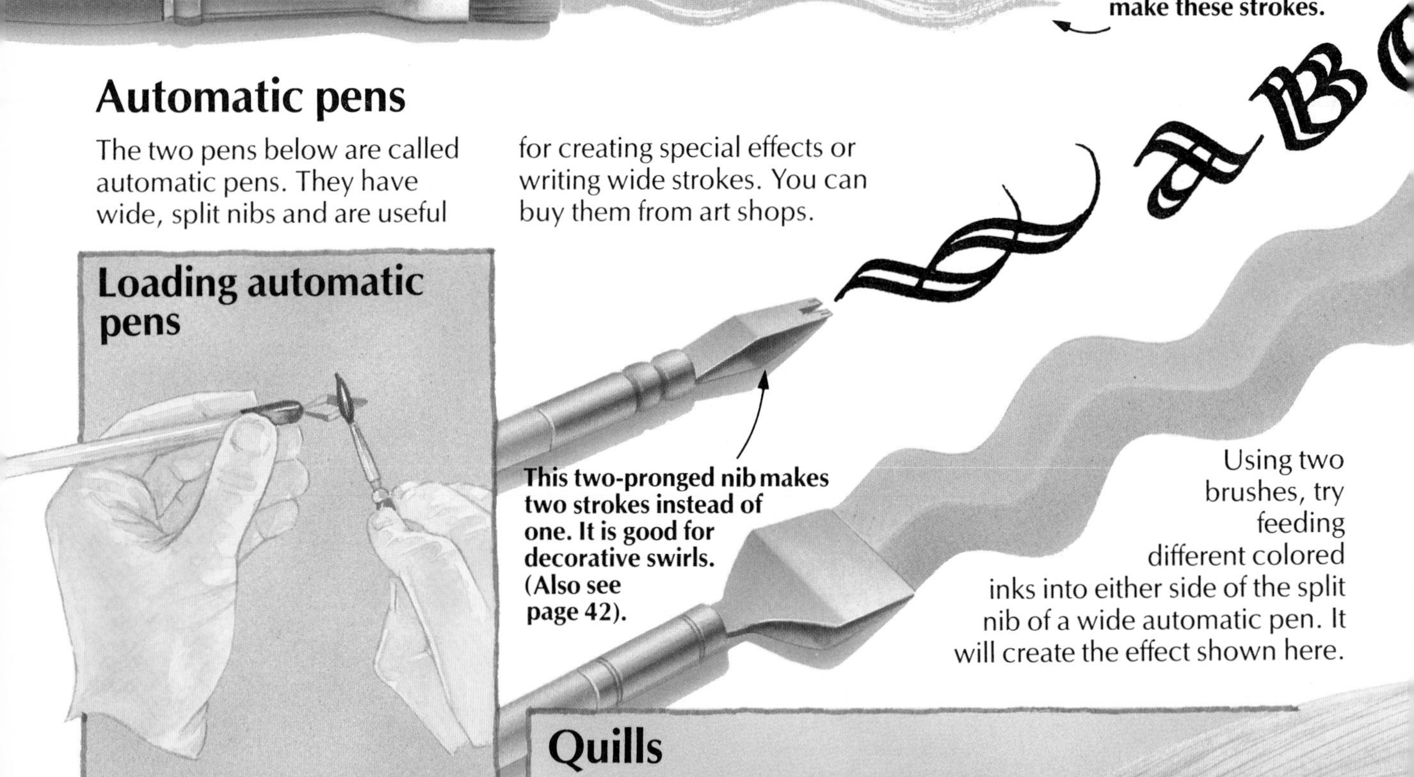

This two-pronged nib makes two strokes instead of one. It is good for decorative swirls. (Also see page 42).

Using two brushes, try feeding different colored inks into either side of the split nib of a wide automatic pen. It will create the effect shown here.

Loading automatic pens

To load your pen, dip a brush in ink and wipe it against the inside bottom edge of the nib on both sides. Ink will collect behind the writing-edge.

Quills

Quills are pens made from birds' feathers. Cutting a quill yourself is very tricky. There are books that give precise instructions if you want to have a go (see page 47).

Some art shops sell ready-cut quills, like this one.

Making your own pens

Here are two simple writing tools you can make yourself. Take great care when using a craft knife. Always place the object on a cutting surface and cut away from your fingers.

Bamboo pens

Bamboo canes were first made into pens thousands of years ago. You can make one with a piece of medium-width garden cane about 10cm long.

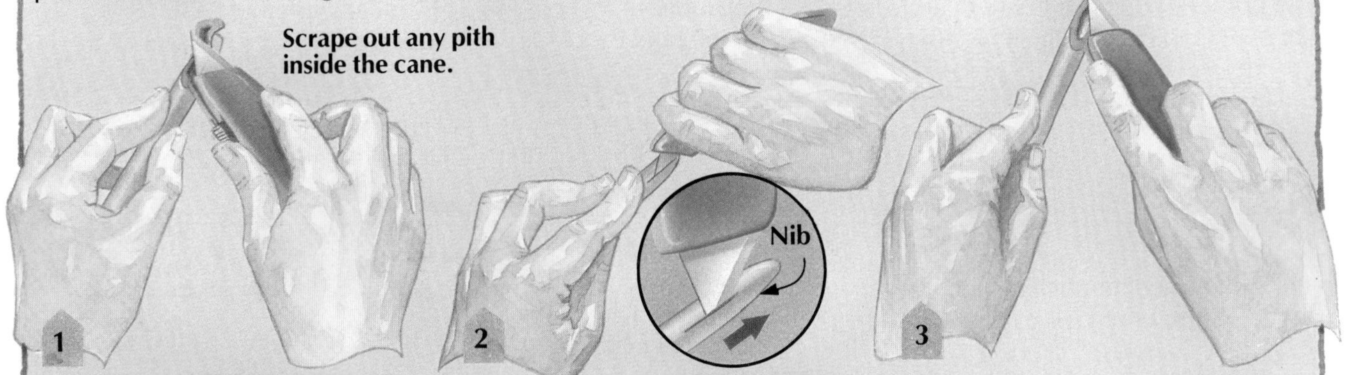
Scrape out any pith inside the cane.
Nib
1
2
3

1. Lay the cane flat on your drawing board. Hold your knife slanting away from you and slice 3cm off the tip.

2. Rest the end of the cane on the edge of your drawing board. Cut a slit about 1cm long down the middle of it.

3. Trim off the last 2mm of the nib. Load your cane with plenty of ink with a brush and it is ready to write with.

Balsa pens

A sheet of balsa wood 10cm wide and 0.5cm thick will make several calligraphy 'pens'. You can buy it from most craft shops quite inexpensively.

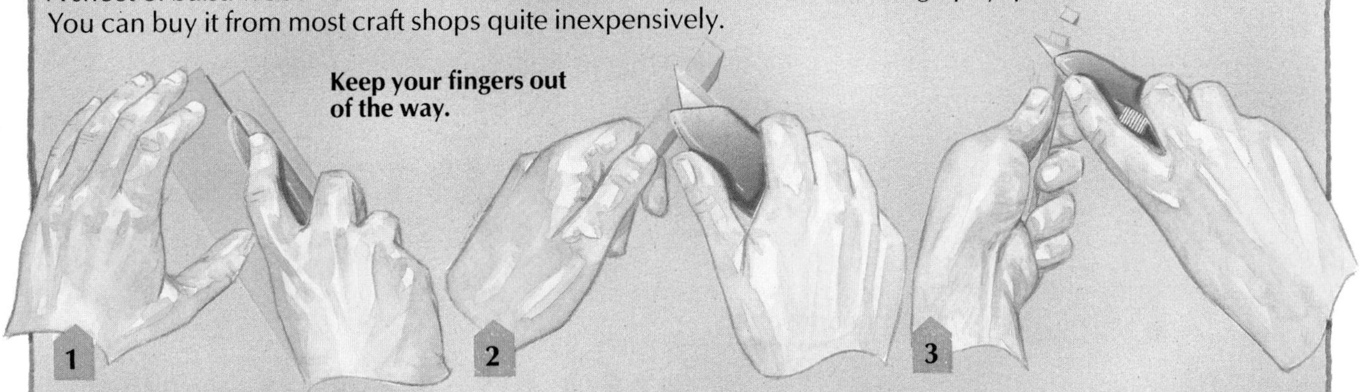
Keep your fingers out of the way.
1
2
3

1. Holding a ruler firmly down on the balsa wood sheet, cut strips of different widths with your craft knife.

2. Cut triangular slices off both sides of one end of each strip. This makes a sharp v-shaped tip.

3. Cut 2mm off the sharpened end. Dip your balsa pen straight into ink or paint to write.

These letters were written with a thin balsa pen.
Cut notches out of a wide balsa strip. Use it to make a background like this.
CAFE

DESIGNING AN ALPHABET

You don't just have to use the lettering styles in this book. Here you can find out how to adapt them, or design a completely new alphabet yourself.

Changing letters

You can use some of the techniques you have learned in this book to change the look of a lettering style.

Here are three ways you can adapt letters.

1

You can use different nibs and x-heights to change the letter's weight (see pages 12-13).

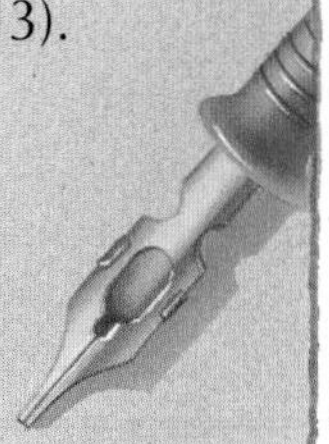

These Foundational letters were written with a narrow nib.

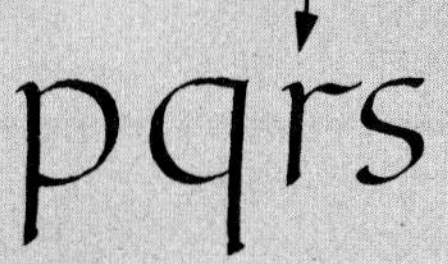
pqrs

2

Try writing with a different tool, such as a brush instead of a pen.

These Uncials were written with a medium calligraphy brush.

pqR

3

You can exaggerate some features of the letters, or add extra strokes.

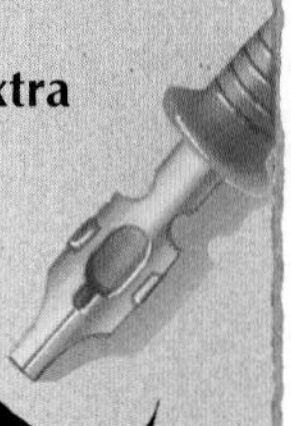

These Italic letters have extra strokes called swashes.

PQR

Your own alphabet

Here are the steps used to create the alphabet at the bottom of the page. You can follow them to invent an alphabet of your own.

1 Fit a wide nib, such as a 1 ½, into your calligraphy pen. You can try out other nibs later if you want to.

2 Choose the look you want your alphabet to have. Then think about what features will achieve it.

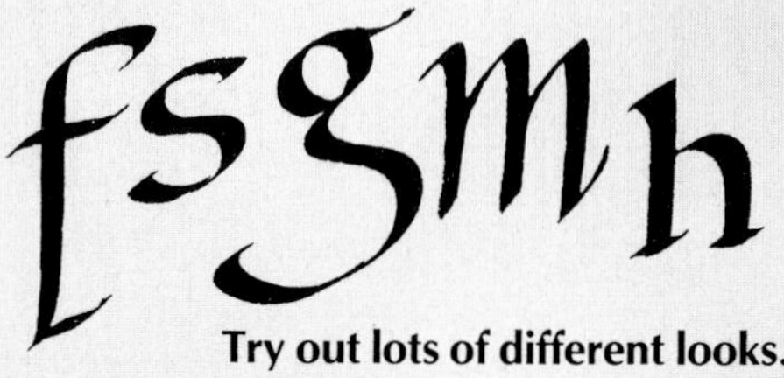
fsgmh

Try out lots of different looks.

O

This 'O' is the basic shape for the alphabet below.

8O

3 Decide on the shape of your 'O' first. This will affect the shape of every other letter in your alphabet.

4 Write your alphabet out in the groups of letters below. You will need to vary the pen angle for the diagonal group to make the letters of your alphabet look consistent.

Narrow letters

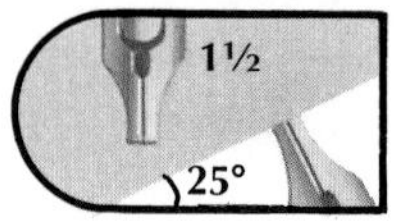
1½
25°

I L E F J K B
P R S

Round letters

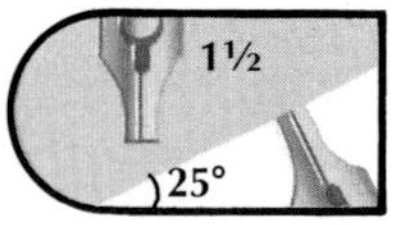
1½
25°

O Q D C G

Rectangular letters

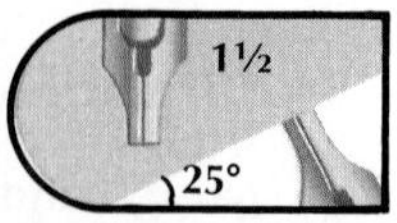
1½
25°

H T U Z

Hold your nib at less of an angle to make this stroke.

Diagonal letters

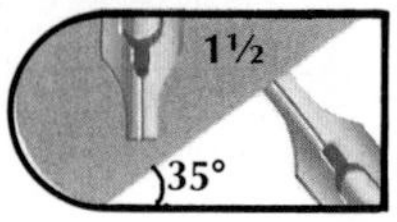
1½
35°

A M N V W
X Y

Personal stationery

You could use your alphabet to personalize some stationery with your name and address. There are some other ideas for decorating your own writing paper and envelopes on pages 52-53.

PAUL LAYNE
27, ASH DRIVE
DENBURY
1
2
3

1. Write out your name and address several times in your alphabet. The letters can be any size you like.

2. Use the cut and paste method on page 15 to try out different layouts on top of a sheet of writing paper.

3. When you have chosen a layout, rule some lines the right distance apart and write the calligraphy.

Logos

You could make an attractive design, or logo, out of your initials written in your alphabet. You can use it on your stationery.

Rubber stamps

You can cut letters into an eraser to make a stamp. On pages 58-59 there are some ideas for decorating giftwrap using a homemade rubber stamp.

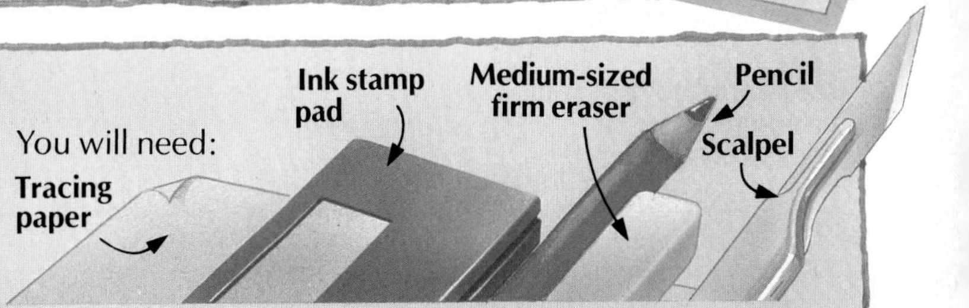
You will need:
Tracing paper
Ink stamp pad
Medium-sized firm eraser
Pencil
Scalpel

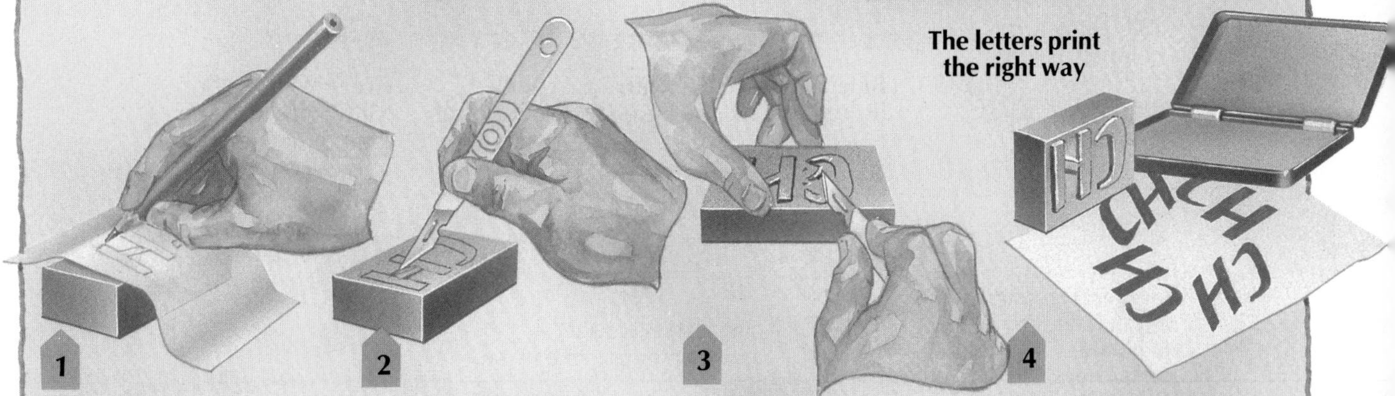
The letters print the right way
1
2
3
4

1. Write the logo on tracing paper with a soft pencil. Turn the sheet over. Use a hard pencil to trace it backwards onto the eraser.

2. Cut around the outline of the letters with a scalpel. Angle the blade outward from the letter strokes slightly.

3. Gradually slice away the eraser around each letter until they are left standing about 2mm above the surface.

4. Press the raised letters onto the ink stamp, and then onto some paper. If the letters are not clear, trim any rough edges carefully.

Calligraphy and Color

There are lots of ways you can make your calligraphy colorful. Some ideas for colored letters and backgrounds are shown here.

Color choices

It's worth spending time choosing colors and trying different combinations.

The colors you choose combine with the lettering style to create the 'look' of each piece of work.

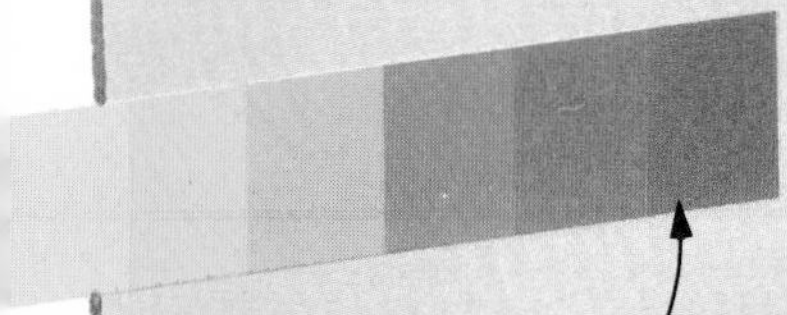

These 'warm' colors create a passionate, fiery, or exciting feeling.

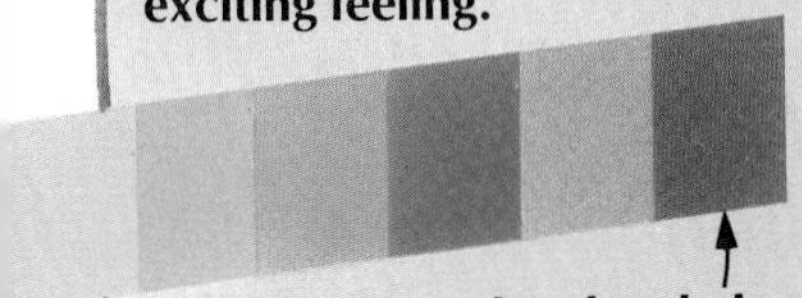

These 'cool' colors help create a calm, peaceful feeling.

These two very different colors make a striking impact.

ac

Pale letters on a dark background and dark letters on a paler background look dramatic.

Colors that are only slightly different give this soft effect.

Writing with gouache

You can use gouache paint for writing calligraphy. Art shops sell a selection of colors in tubes or jars.

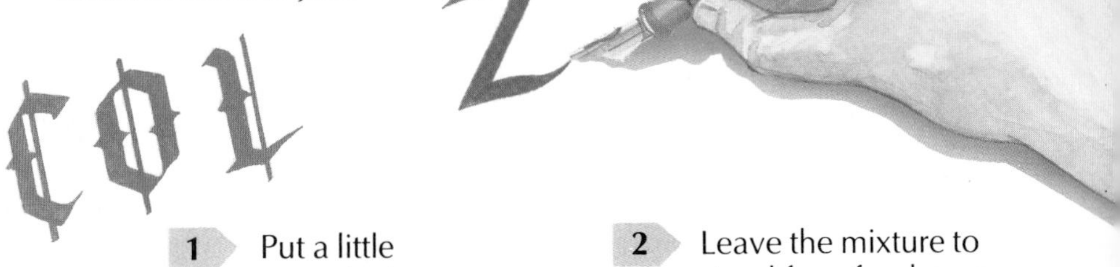
COLZ

1 Put a little gouache into a small jar. Add a little water and mix until it is a creamy consistency.

2 Leave the mixture to stand for a few hours. Load it into your calligraphy pen with a brush.

Changing colors

Try loading your pen with a slightly different color gouache after writing a few letters. Don't wash it out between colors. Mix your paints in a ice cube tray, starting at the top row, then going back to the second.

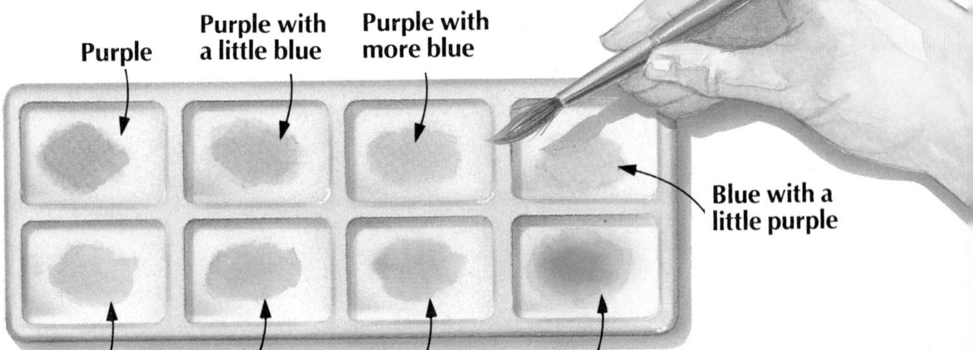
Purple
Purple with a little blue
Purple with more blue
Blue with a little purple
Blue with a little green
Blue with more green
Equal amounts of green and blue
Green with a little blue

abcdefghi

The letters would look something like these.

Colored inks

You can use colored waterproof inks straight from the jar, but they can produce patchy lettering and may clog your pen.

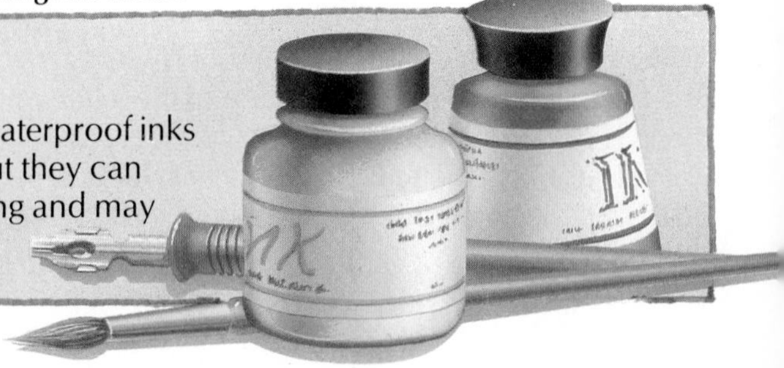
INK
INK

A color wash

You could try brushing watered down gouache or watercolor paint over white paper to make a subtly colored background. This is called a color wash.

1 Float the paper in water for about a minute. Tape it flat on your drawing board with brown gummed tape from an art shop. Let the paper dry.

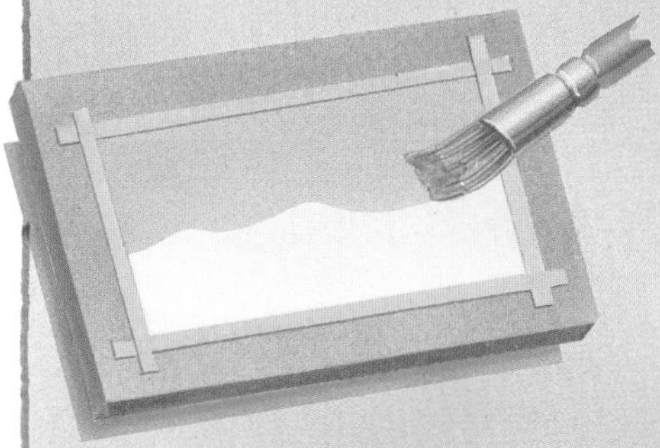

2 Brush the paper with water and then with watered-down paint. The more watery the paint mixture, the paler the background will be.

3 When the paper is dry, write the calligraphy. Choose a strong color so that the letters stand out clearly.

Washing over wax

You can add a color wash over calligraphy letters if you write them with a rubbed-down wax crayon, as shown on page 5. The example below was written with a white crayon.

1 Using your rubbed-down crayon, write some calligraphy letters on a sheet of white paper.

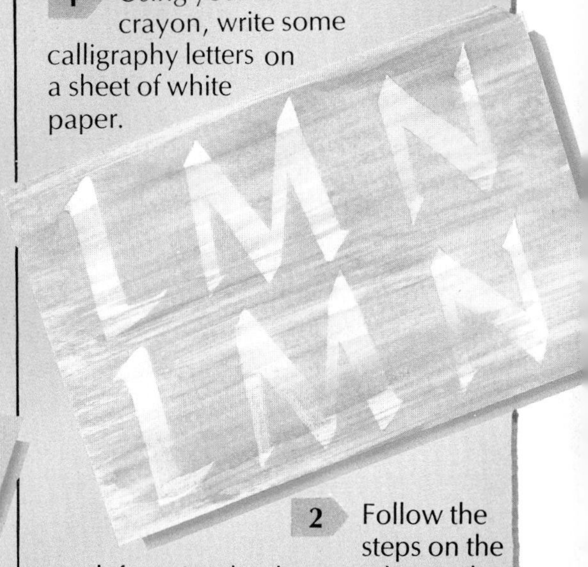

2 Follow the steps on the left to give the sheet a color wash.

Invisible letters

You can create interesting effects by using masking fluid from an art shop. See page 59 for another technique which shows you how to sponge ink over the fluid.

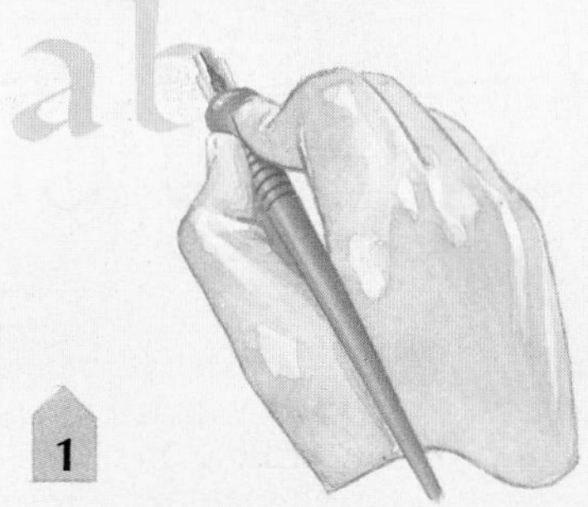

1

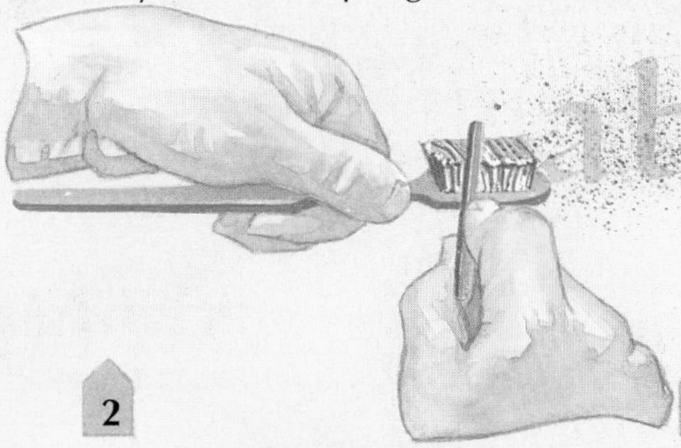

2

3

Pour some masking fluid into a saucer. Load your pen with fluid, using a brush, and write some letters.

Dip an old toothbrush in paint, hold it over the letters and gently pull a matchstick along the top of the bristles.

Rub the letters with your fingertip. They will 'appear' in the spattered paint where the fluid 'masked' the paper.

STENCILS AND RUBBINGS

Letter shapes can be cut out as well as written. Here you can find out how to use cut-out calligraphy letters to make stencils and letter rubbings.

Making stencils

You can make a stencil using any of the lettering styles in this book. It is best to use waxed stencil paper from an art shop, but thin card will do.

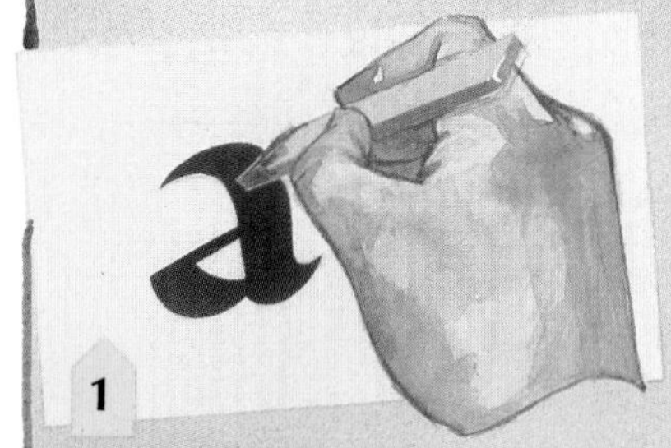
a
1

Write some large letters on layout paper. Then, go around the outline of each one with a pencil on tracing paper.

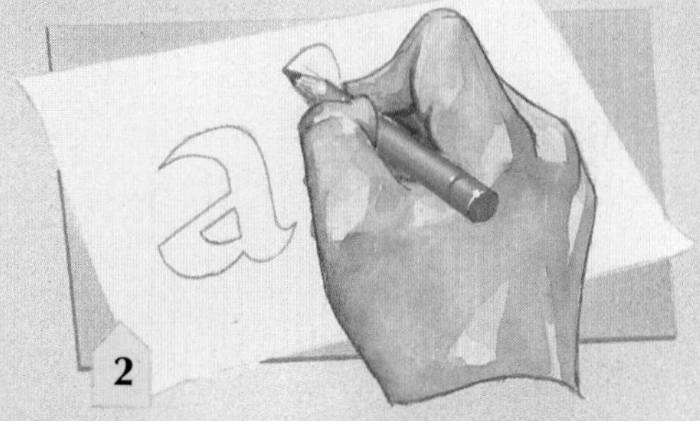
a
2

Trace the letters onto your stencil paper or cardboard. Make thin strokes thicker as it will be easier to cut them out.

Middle piece from letter 'a'.
3

Carefully cut around the letters with a craft knife or scalpel to make a stencil. Keep the 'middles' that fall out.

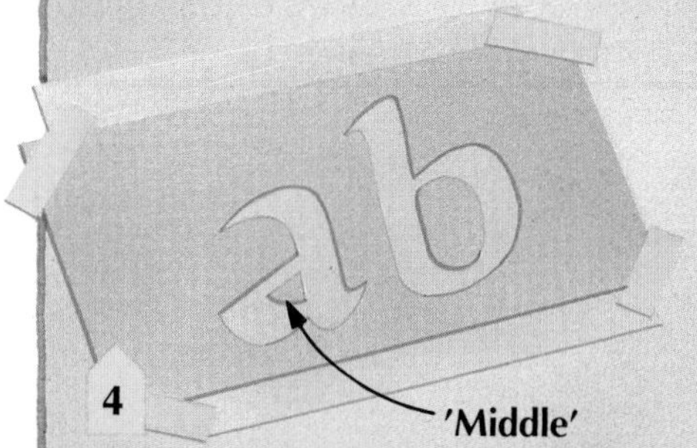
ab
4
'Middle'

Tape your stencil to a piece of layout paper with masking tape. Stick any 'middles' in place with glue or rubber cement.

5
Be careful not to move the 'middle'.

Color through the 'gaps' in your stencil with pencil, crayons or a small piece of cotton wool dipped in paint.

b
6

Carefully take the stencil and middles off the paper. Keep them so you can build up a 'library' of stencils.

Stylish stencils

You can use stencils to decorate all kinds of objects. Use ceramic paint, which you can buy from most craft shops, to decorate a mug (see pages 62-63) or a plate (see pages 70-71).

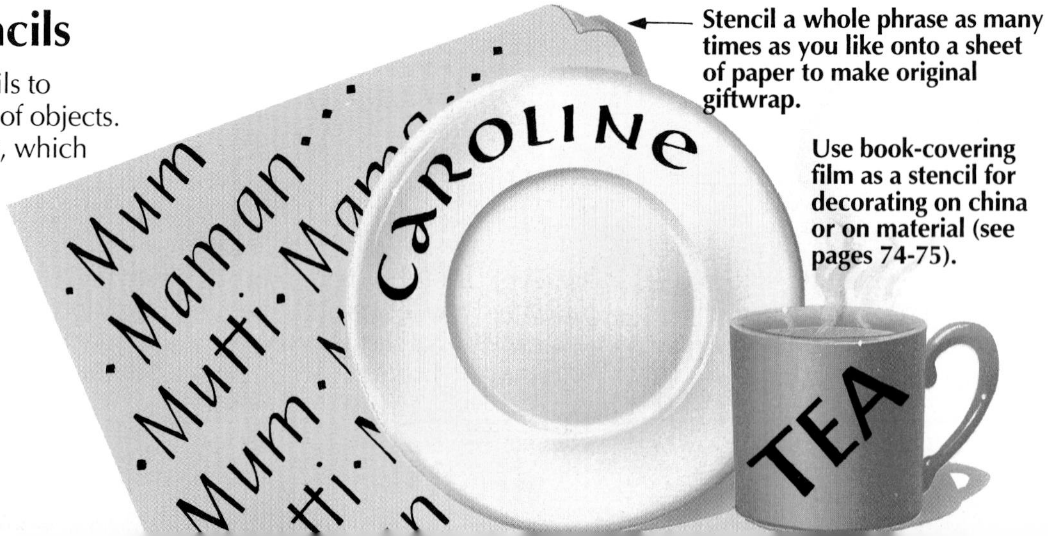
Stencil a whole phrase as many times as you like onto a sheet of paper to make original giftwrap.
Use book-covering film as a stencil for decorating on china or on material (see pages 74-75).
·Mum
·Maman·
·Mutti·
·Mum·
CAROLINE
TEA

Letter rubbings

Try putting paper over your calligraphy stencils or cut-out letters. Then rub across them with a soft pencil or wax crayon. This is called taking a rubbing.

Rub all around the letter, as shown here.
1
2
3

1. Cut the letters you want out of thin cardboard, as on the page opposite. This time, you will use the pieces you cut out.

2. Stick the letters onto a piece of cardboard with rubber cement in any layout you choose. This makes your rubbing board.

3. Put a piece of layout paper over the rubbing board. Gently rub a crayon or soft pencil over the whole sheet to make a rubbing.

Making gift tags

You could make gift tags with letter rubbings on them. Punch a hole and thread a ribbon through each one to tie it to a gift. Use thin cardboard as it is stronger than paper and should still make clear rubbings. See pages 58-59.

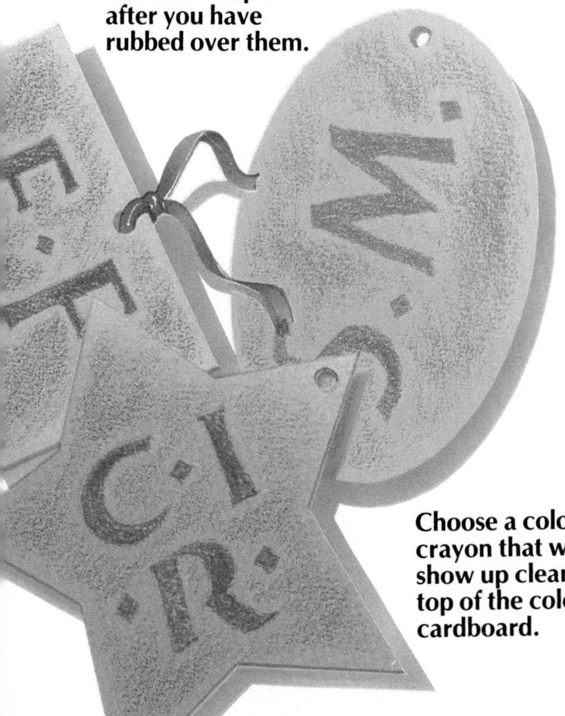

Cut your tags into different shapes after you have rubbed over them.
Choose a color crayon that will show up clearly on top of the colored cardboard.

Colorful collage

Try doing a large poster made up of a collage of calligraphy letter rubbings.

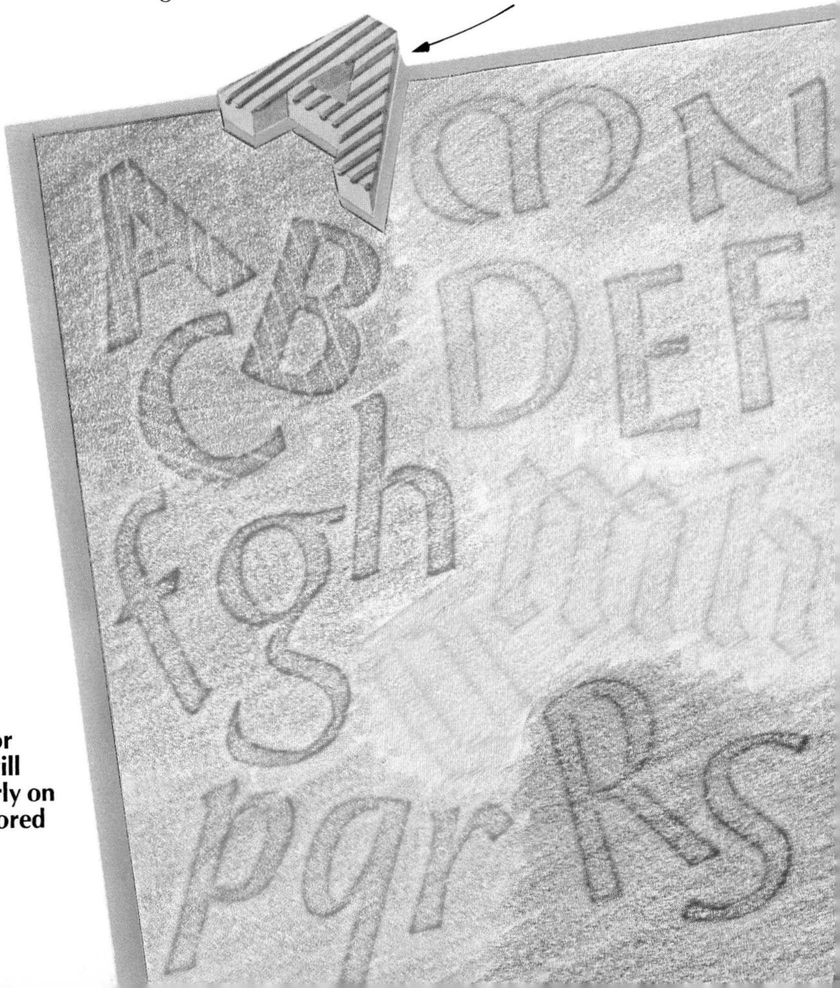

This letter was cut from corrugated cardboard to make a textured rubbing.

EMBOSSING AND INCISING

Two more advanced techniques you can use with calligraphy letters are shown here. They are called embossing and incising.

Embossing

Embossed letters are not written, but 'molded' in paper. It is easy to emboss paper to make your own stationery (see pages 52-53).

You will need:
A thin sheet of cardboard.
A round-ended paintbrush.
A sheet of layout paper.
A craft knife or scalpel.
A sheet of medium-thickness cartridge paper.
A soft and a hard pencil.

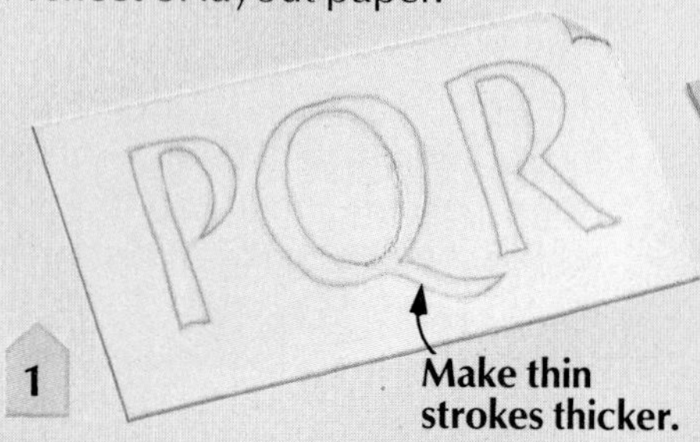
PQR
1
Make thin strokes thicker.

Draw the outline of some large letters on a sheet of layout paper with a soft pencil.

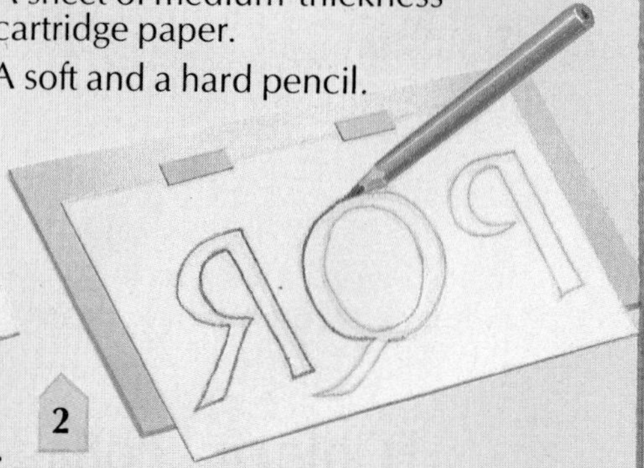
2

Turn the paper over. Tape it onto the thin cardboard. Go over the backward letters with a hard pencil.

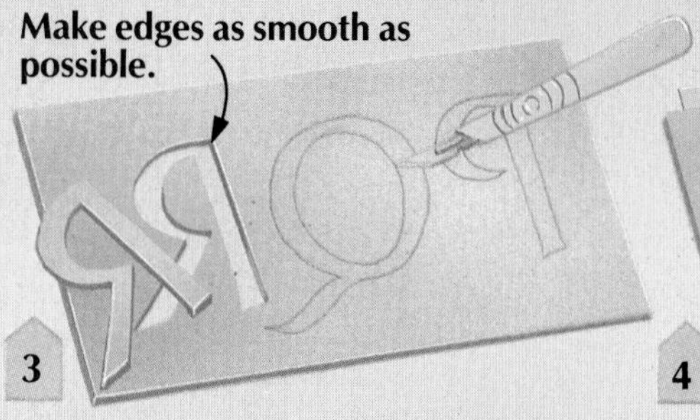
Make edges as smooth as possible.
3

The letters will be backwards on the cardboard. Cut them out with a sharp craft knife or scalpel.

4

Glue the cardboard on top of a second sheet of cardboard. Then lay the thick paper over them.

Don't rub too hard or the paper might tear.
5

Gently rub the paper into the letter 'molds' with the rounded end of your paintbrush.

PQR
6

Turn the paper over. Your embossed letters should be raised above the surface of the paper.

Embossing effects

Embossed letters look very sophisticated. Here are some ways you could use them.

Invitations are often embossed.
Embossed writing paper is very stylish.
RSVP
This stands for 'répondez s'il vous plaît', or 'please reply', in French.
E·M·M·A
JANE
AUSTEN
Make an embossed paper cover to go around a book.

Light and shade

Embossed letters cast soft shadows. Hang some embossing on a wall and try lighting it from different angles to get the best effect.

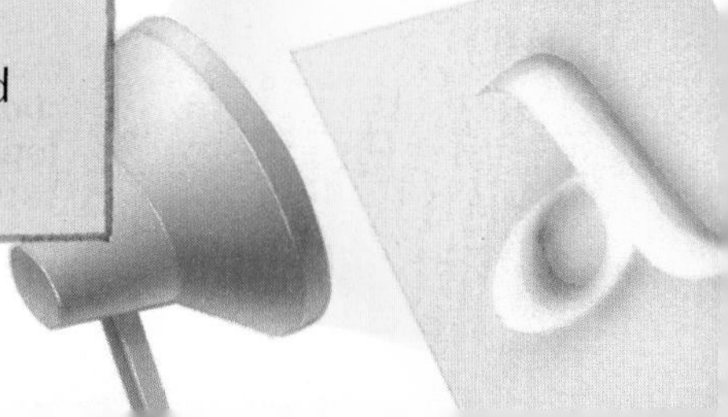

Incising

Incised letters are carved into something solid, such as stone or clay. You can incise most calligraphy styles, but Roman capitals are good to start with as they produce the best effects.

You will need:

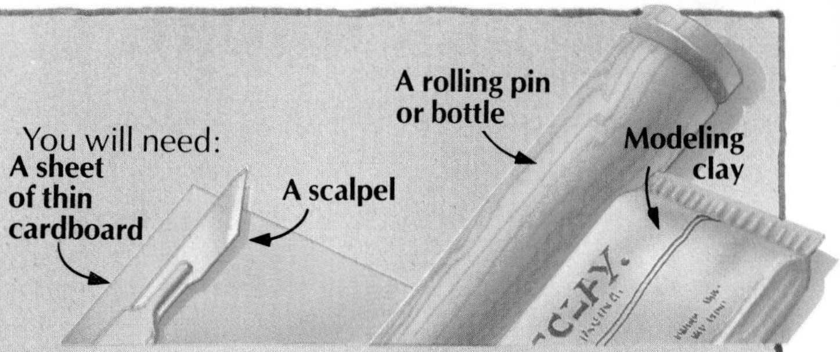
A sheet of thin cardboard
A scalpel
A rolling pin or bottle
Modeling clay

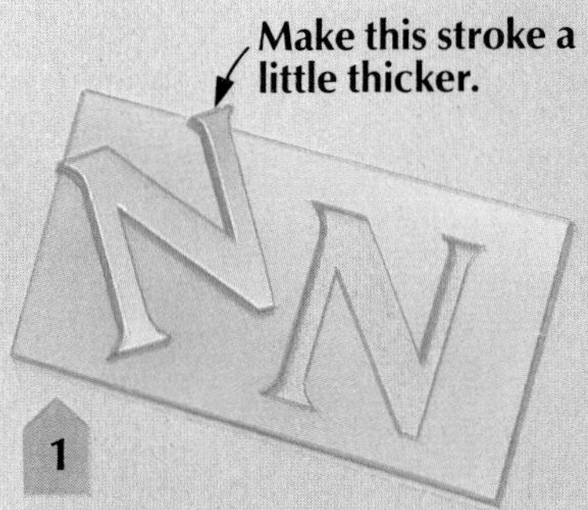
Make this stroke a little thicker.
1

Draw the outline of a letter in pencil on thin cardboard. Thicken thin strokes, then cut it out.

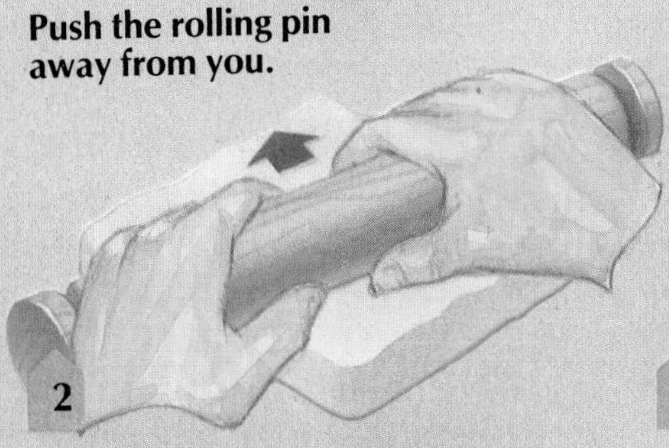
Push the rolling pin away from you.
2

Knead the clay until it is smooth and bubble-free. Roll it on a flat surface until it is about 3cm thick.

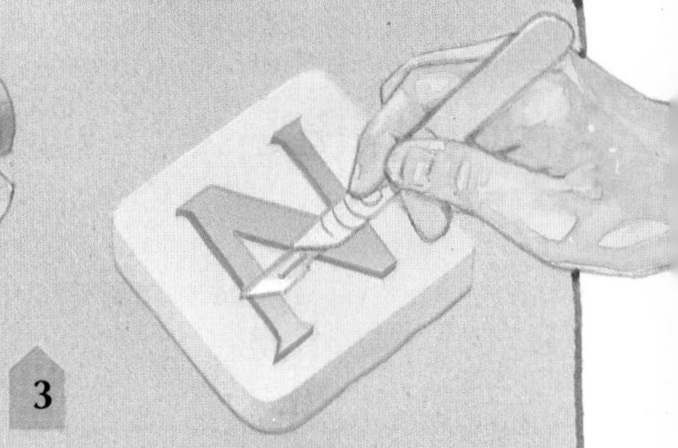
3

Lay the cardboard letter on the clay. Go around it lightly with a scalpel, then take the letter off.

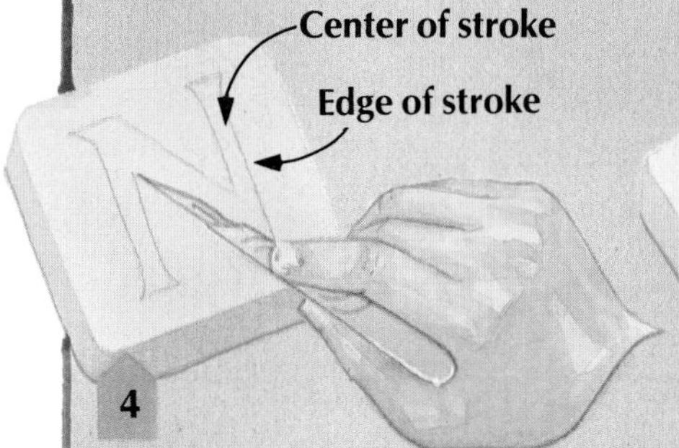
Center of stroke
Edge of stroke
4

Keeping the scalpel blade at a constant angle, cut in from one edge of the letter stroke towards the center of the stroke.

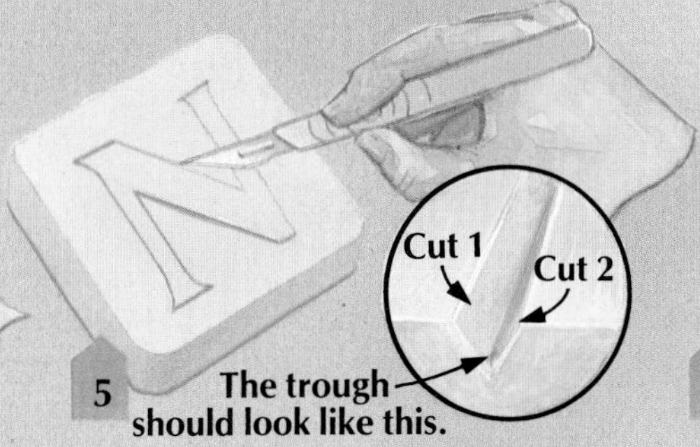
Cut 1
Cut 2
5
The trough should look like this.

Cut in from the other side to meet the first scalpel cut. Lift out the excess clay to leave a v-shaped trough for each stroke.

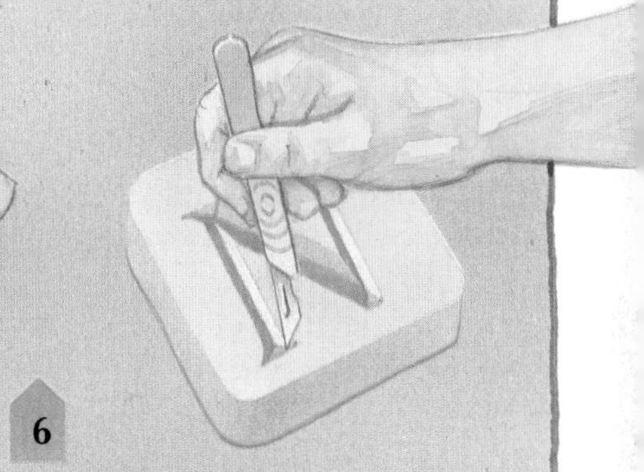
6

To make serifs, cut across the top of the stroke with the scalpel and ease the clay out. Make the point with the tip of the blade.

Clay tiles

You could carve some letters or numbers into a clay tile to put outside your house or on a door.

When the clay is dry, you could paint the tile, or just the incised letters, with waterproof enamel paint.

Eva
U.F.
52

You can find these numbers to trace on page 45

These shapes were made from leftover clay. Brush them with a little water to make them stick onto the tile.

Careers and Calligraphy

Becoming a professional calligrapher is not easy. You will need to do some further training. Most calligraphers don't work full-time for one company but take on projects from different companies.

Further study

You can study calligraphy on full-time or part-time courses. Write to the addresses on page 47 for details.

- There are a few specialist calligraphy courses. You don't need specific qualifications to take one, but must show promise as a calligrapher.

Full-time courses

- You can study calligraphy as one option on some Graphic Design courses. Entry requirements vary, but it would be useful to study Art or Technical Drawing.

Part-time courses

- Many areas run calligraphy evening classes, summer schools or correspondence courses.

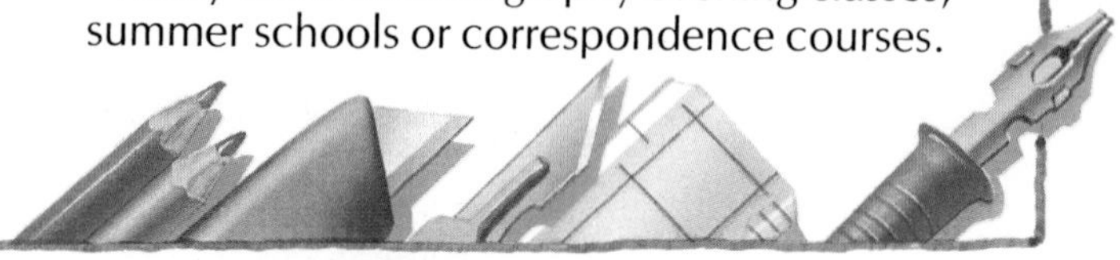

Preparing your portfolio

Select pieces of your work that show off your calligraphy skills best. They make up what is called your portfolio.

You can buy a flat case to keep your work in, also called a portfolio. On page 47 you can find out how to make a simpler one yourself.

Portfolio
Merry Christmas
The leaves fluttered in the wind restlessly

Getting work

Your first job is always the hardest to find. After that, customers may use you again or recommend you to others. Here are some ways to look for work.

- Make a list of possible clients in your area, such as schools, small businesses or card shops.
- Call their receptionist to find out the best person for you to contact at each one.

Companies need headed stationery.
·ALPHA·GRAPHICS·
Certificate of merit awarded to Elizabeth Smith
Schools often award certificates that are written in calligraphy.
TAXI
0-372-4160
Business card

- Write to them, saying you are starting out as a calligrapher. Offer to visit them to show them your portfolio.
- When they see your portfolio, draw their attention to pieces that are especially relevant to their needs.
- If they ask you to do some work for them, you can find out how to go about it on the page opposite.

A professional job

Below are the steps a professional calligrapher takes to design a calendar for a local company.

1 The client tells the calligrapher exactly what the job involves. These details form what is called a brief for the job.

2 If both are happy to go ahead, the client asks, or commissions him to do it. They agree on a delivery date and a fee.

3 In the studio, the calligrapher makes small sketches of possible layouts for the piece. These are called 'thumbnails'.

4 The calligrapher tries out several styles, weights and sizes of calligraphy letters. Cut and paste helps him find the best layout.

5 The calligrapher discusses his ideas and thumbnails with the client. They select the layout they feel fulfils the brief best.

6 The calligrapher assembles the equipment for the job. In a quiet room to help concentration, he writes the finished piece.

7 The work is delivered to the client. If it is on time and is satisfactory, the calligrapher is paid the agreed fee.

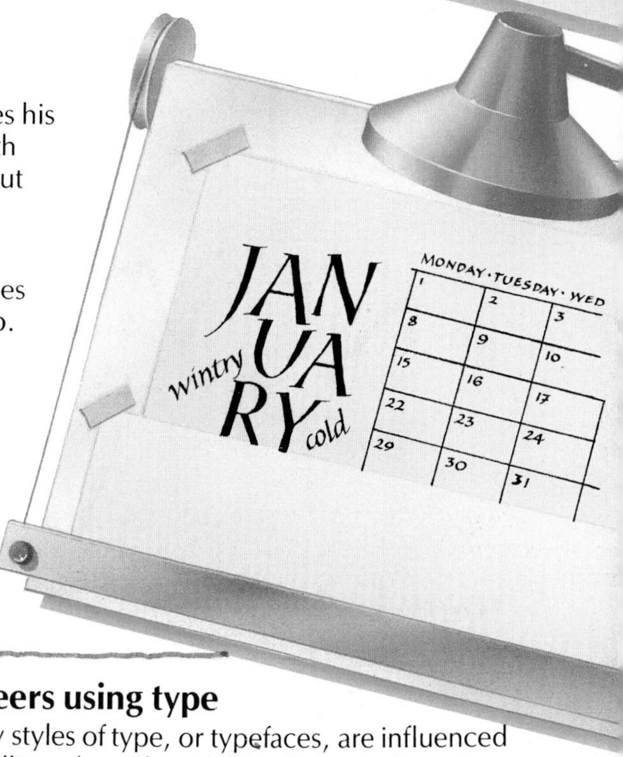

Other careers

The lettering skills you learn while doing calligraphy can be useful in other careers too.

Signwriting

Many signs outside shops and restaurants are hand-painted by professional signwriters. The equipment is slightly different from a calligrapher's, but the skills are very similar.

This hand-painted sign is for a French restaurant.

Careers using type

Many styles of type, or typefaces, are influenced by calligraphy styles. Skill in choosing the right one could be useful if you want to work in publishing, journalism or advertising.

This typeface is closely based on the Gothic calligraphy style. It helps give this menu a traditional, old-fashioned feel.

This typeface gives this shampoo an elegant, feminine appeal. It is called an Italic typeface. The letters lean to the right, like calligraphy Italics.

This plain, sans serif type could be used in children's books as it is easy to read.

Alphabets to copy • 1

On the next five pages, you will find ten more alphabets to try. There are suggestions on where to use them in your calligraphy, too.

Roman capitals

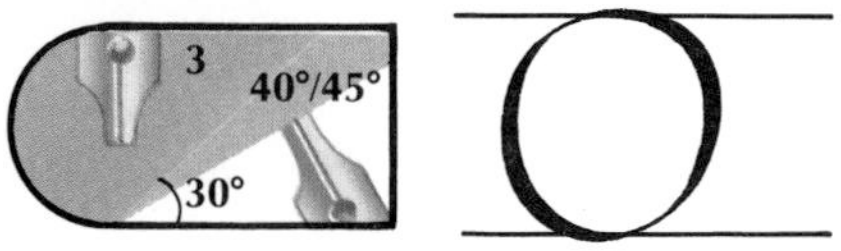
3
40°/45°
30°

The Roman capitals made by following the skeleton letters on page 8 should look like the letters below. They go well with most styles of minuscules. You can add serifs or leave them sans serif (see page 9). These letters are sans serif.

ABCDEFGHIJ
KLMNOPQRS
TUVWXYZ

Ornate Gothic

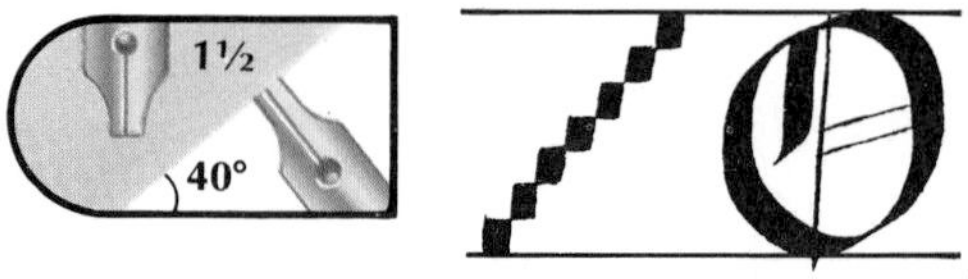
1½
40°

These Gothic capitals are more ornate than those on page 16. They will also take longer to write as they have more strokes. Use them with the minuscules also on page 16.

Italic capitals

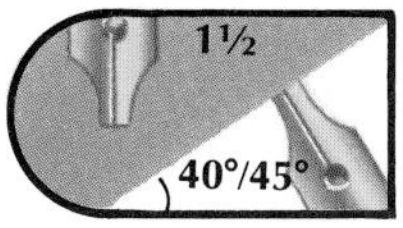

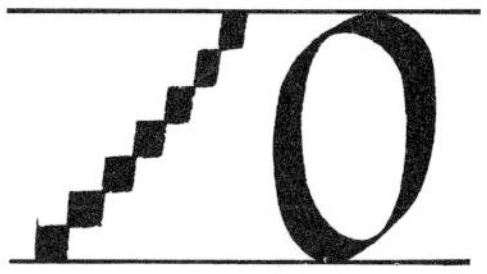

Italic capitals are most commonly used with Italic minuscules as they both lean 5° to the right (see page 18). They can be effective when combined with other styles, too.

Swash capitals

These letters are called Swash Italic capitals, as they have added strokes called swashes (see page 18). Keep them short or they will clash with other lines of text.

Filled Versals

The Versal strokes shown on page 20 should make letters like those below. They go well with most minuscule styles. Try writing them with a wide brush for posters.

Alphabets to copy • 2

The six minuscule alphabets on this page have very different 'looks'. They are written with a variety of calligraphy tools. Each one creates a different effect.

Carolingian minuscules

The letters below are called Carolingian minuscules. They were the first real small letters (see page 2). They look best when used with large Uncials or Versals.

Split nib alphabet

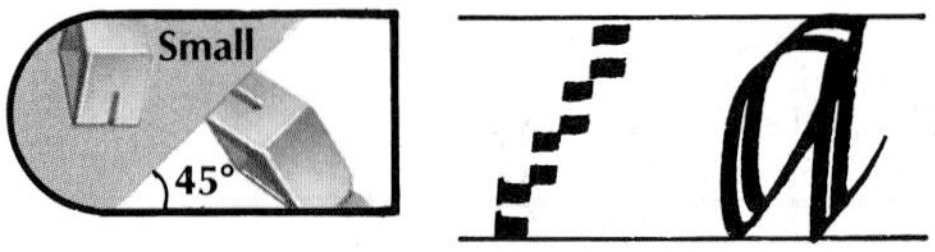

The letters below were written with an automatic pen with a split nib, called a scroll pen. They are based on Italics, so follow the strokes as shown on page 18.

Handwriting alphabet

This is an Italic handwriting alphabet. It shows how each letter should be joined to other letters. Try writing the alphabet joined together as shown here to increase your speed and develop a smooth style.

Brush alphabet

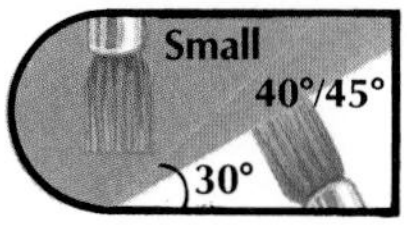

These Foundational letters (see page 11), were written with a small calligraphy brush dipped in watered-down ink.

Two original alphabets

The two alphabets below were designed by a calligrapher called Solos Solou. They both have an 'Eastern' feel.

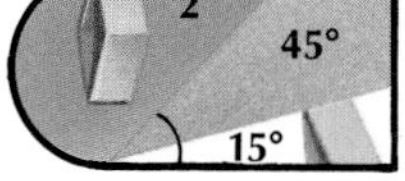

This alphabet was written with a narrow automatic pen. Twist the nib to form a steeper angle (45°) to make the vertical strokes get thinner at the bottom.

Ascenders are twice as high as the body of each letter.

Alphabets to copy • 3

You could trace off the outlines of the two alphabets on this page and use them for illumination, embossing, posters or stencilling.

Outline alphabet

The thin strokes of these outline letters have been made slightly thicker. This makes them easier to trace around and cut out.

ABCDEFG
HIJKLMN
OPQRSTU
VWXYZ

Type alphabet

This is a style of type, or typeface, called Optima. Here it is printed very big and bold (heavyweight) to make it easier to trace around.

It was designed by a calligrapher called Hermann Zapf. Optima letters have thick and thin strokes, like calligraphy letters.

If you look closely, you will see that all the type in this book is Optima, used in different sizes and weights.

Thick stroke

abcdefghi

Thin stroke

jklmnopq
rstuvwxyz

Numbers and patterns

Here are some numbers and more border patterns, to use in your calligraphy.

Chinese numbers

Write these Chinese numbers with a bamboo brush (see page 26).

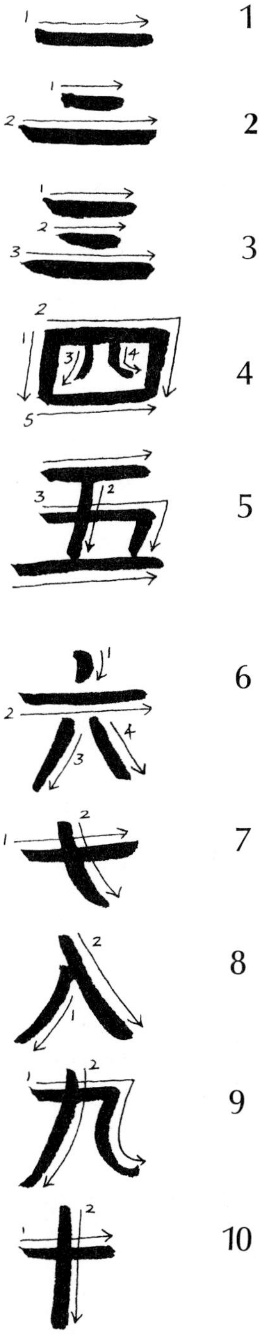
1
2
3
4
5
6
7
8
9
10

Arabic numbers

The numbers used in most Western countries are called Arabic numbers. You can use them with all the calligraphy styles in this book. Make them the same size and weight as the letters in the piece.

Continental seven

Italic numbers

For Italic calligraphy, make the numbers slightly narrower, like the ones shown here. They should also lean 5° to the right.

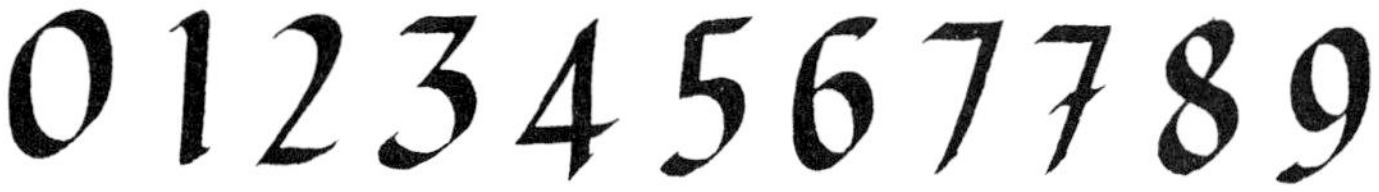

Punctuation

You can use these puncuation marks with all the calligraphy styles in this book.

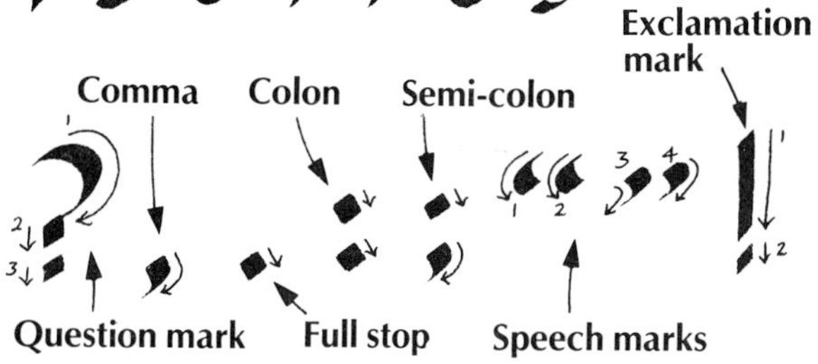
Comma
Colon
Semi-colon
Exclamation mark
Question mark
Full stop
Speech marks

Patterned borders

These borders were made with a calligraphy pen. Choose one which goes well with your lettering style (see pages 22 for some hints). There are some more borders on page 67.

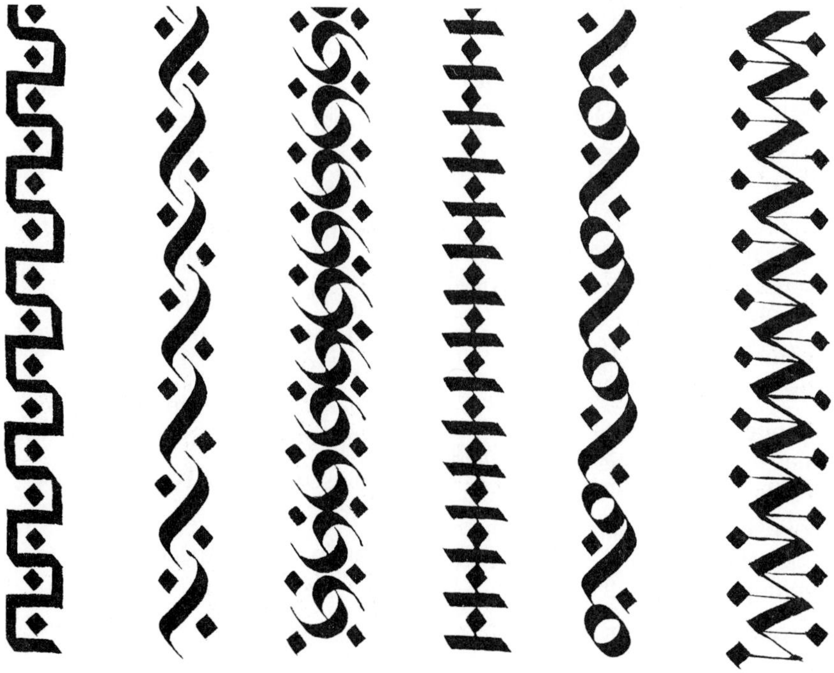

Glossary

aligned left: each line of text starts at the same point on the left-hand **margin**.

aligned right: each line ends at the same point on the right-hand **margin**. They start at different points on the left.

arched letter: letter which has an arch that springs away from the central **stroke** or **stem**.

ascender: **stroke** going up from the main **body** of a **lower-case letter**, or **minuscule**.

asymmetrical layout: lines of text placed irregularly on the page.

base line: line on which capital letters are written and the **body** of a **minuscule** rests. Also called the **writing line**.

basic shape: the letter which influences the shape of all other letters in a callgraphy style. Usually an 'o'.

body: main part of a **minuscule**, which forms the letter's **x-height**.

brief: details of a piece of work, given to an artist by a client.

built-up letter: a letter in which each part is made up of several **strokes**.

burnish: to make something shine, such as the **gilding**.

capital letter: large or **upper-case letter**. Also called a **majuscule**.

centred layout: lines of **text** balanced on both sides of the middle of the page.

character: a single letter. In Chinese script, each character represents a whole idea.

commission: to ask a calligrapher to do some work for an agreed fee.

condense: to make letters smaller, narrower or re-arrange them slightly so that they take up less space.

crossbar: stroke across the upper part of the letters 't' and 'f' and the middle of 'A' and 'H'.

cross-hatching: shading with parallel or criss-crossed lines.

cursive writing: writing in which some letters are joined together for speed. Usually handwriting.

cut and paste: technique of cutting paper with **text** on it into strips and sticking them down in different **layouts** to judge their effect.

descender: **stroke** going down from the main **body** of a **lower-case letter** (**minuscule**).

diagonal letter: letter which has **strokes** which go in a diagonal direction, such as 'z','v','w' and 'x'.

emboss: to shape paper in some areas by pressing it into or over a mould.

flourish: extra, decorative **stroke**.

gilding: covering a surface with a thin layer of gold, or gold colour.

grain (paper): the direction in which most fibres lie in a sheet of paper.

grid: framework of lines and curves on which letters are based.

guidelines: pencil lines between which calligraphy is written to make sure it is straight.

illumination: decoration of a piece of calligraphy with gold and colour.

incise: to carve letters in a hard substance such as stone or clay.

kneading: squeezing clay to make it smooth and remove air bubbles.

layout: the way **text** and pictures are arranged on a page.

loading (a pen): filling it with ink, usually with a small brush.

logo: specially designed symbol or trademark for a company, product or person.

lower-case letter: small letter or **minuscule.**

majuscule: **capital** or **upper-case letter**.

margin: area of space around a piece of writing.

minuscule: small or **lower-case letter**.

portfolio: flat case for carrying artwork. Also the work inside.

resist: method using two substances that do not mix, such as wax and watercolour paint or masking fluid and gouache paint.

round letter: letter which closely follows the shape of the letter 'o'.

rubbing: the mark or impression left by rubbing wax crayon or a soft pencil over a sheet of paper laid over some **incised** or raised letters.

ruling up: measuring and drawing **guidelines** to write some calligraphy.

sans serif: a letter without **serifs**.

serif: small **stroke** which is added to the beginning and end of some letter **strokes**.

skeleton letter: letter written in its most basic form, with a thin nib or writing tool.

stem: main vertical **stroke** of a letter.

stencil: sheet from which shapes or letters have been cut out. Colour is applied through the gaps onto the surface underneath to re-produce the cut-out shapes.

stroke: part of a letter made by a single pen stroke.

text: writing.

thumbnail: small, rough sketch of a **layout**.

typeface: style of type in printing.

upper-case letter: capital letter or majuscule.

wash: watered-down paint brushed over paper.

weight: relationship between a letter's height (**x-height** for **minuscules**) and the thickness of the nib it is written with.

writing-line: line on which letters are written. Also called the **base line**.

x-height: height of the main **body** of a **minuscule**.

Useful information

If you want to take calligraphy further, there is information you might find useful on this page.

Making a portfolio

A portfolio for carrying your work, as shown on page 39, can be expensive. Here's how to make a simple one from sheets of cardboard.

You will need :

Three sheets of stiff cardboard

A sheet of stiff paper

Some ribbon

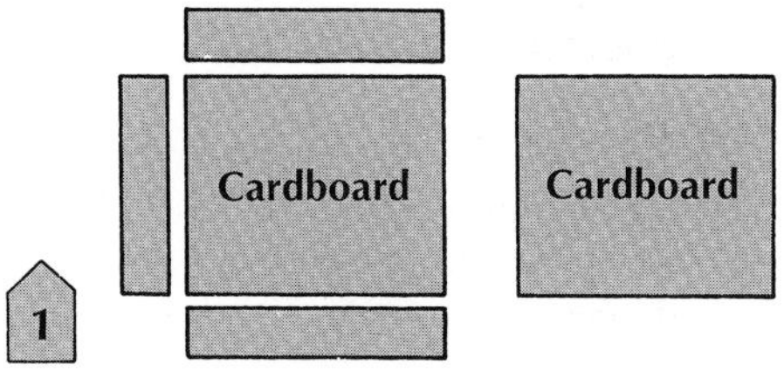

Cut two sheets of the cardboard to the size you need your portfolio to be. Cut three flaps to fit the sides out of the third sheet.

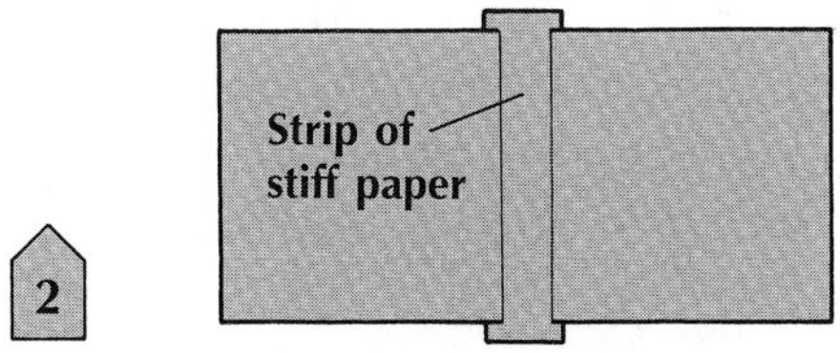

Glue the two sheets to each side of a strip of stiff paper, as shown here. This will act as a hinge for the portfolio.

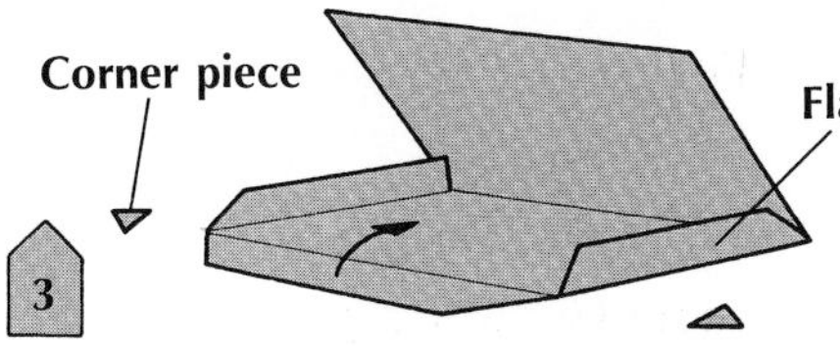

Glue the flaps to the sides of one sheet of cardboard. Cut off their corners and fold them inward.

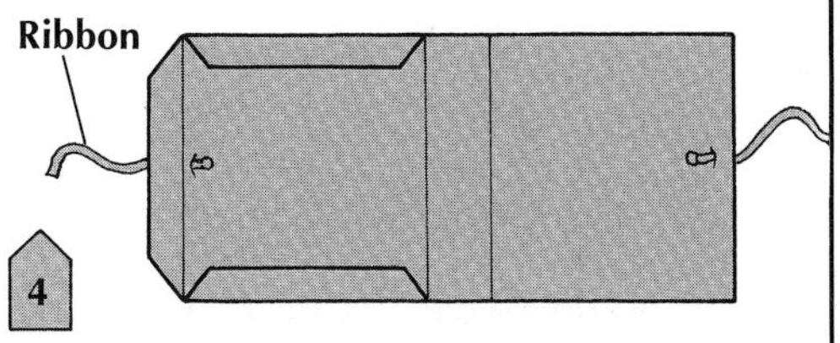

Slit the cardboard where shown here. Thread the ribbon through each slit, glueing about 5mm ($^{2}/_{10}$in) of one end to the cardboard.

Books to read

Creating Letterforms - Rosemary Sassoon and Patricia Lovett (Thames and Hudson).

Creative Calligraphy - Rachel Yallop (Hodder and Stoughton).

Teach Yourself Calligraphy - Patricia Lovett (Hodder and Stoughton).

The Calligrapher's Project Book - Susanne Haines (HarperCollins).

Lettering and Typography - Tony Potter (Usborne).

Creative Lettering and Calligraphy - Peter Halliday (Kingfisher).

Calligraphy Made Easy - Margaret Shepherd (HarperCollins).

Practical Calligraphy - Edited by Mike Darton (Quintet).

The Encyclopedia of Calligraphy Techniques - Diana Hardy Wilson (Headline).

Advanced Calligraphy Techniques - Diana Hoare (Studio Vista).

The Practical Guide to Calligraphy- Rosemary Sassoon (Thames and Hudson)

Learn Lettering and Calligraphy - Gail and Peter Lawther (Macdonald).

Color Calligraphy - Barbara Bundy (Osmiroid International).

Calligraphy, Art and Color - Peter Halliday (Batsford).

Calligraphy Today - Heather Child (A & C Black).

The Calligraphy Source Book - Miriam Stribley (Macdonald).

Calligraphy : The Rhythm of Writing - Satwinder Sehmi (Merehurst Press).

Quill-cutting - See Donald Jackson's piece in **The Calligrapher's Handbook** (A & C Black).

Chinese Calligraphy - Yee Chiang (Harvard University Press).

Chinese Brush Painting - Jane Evans (HarperCollins).

Hebrew Calligraphy - Jay Seth Greenspan (Fodor USA).

Islamic Calligraphy - Yasin Hamid Safadi (Thames and Hudson).

Societies

There are many local societies for calligraphers. Ask at your local library for the address and telephone number of groups in your area. They should be able to give you information about exhibitions and courses. An international society especially for young people who are interested in calligraphy is 'Letters'. They issue a newsletter which is packed with practical ideas, projects and information. They also run workshops for young calligraphers in a variety of locations. For more information send a stamped addressed envelope to 'Letters', Hernewood, Gracious Lane, Sevenoaks, Kent TN13 1TJ, England.

Sun clock
(see pages 68-69)

Zigzag card
(see pages 54-55)

Gift tag
(see pages 58-59)

Terracotta pot
(see pages 66-67)

Interlocking giftboxes
(see pages 60-61)

Part two

CALLIGRAPHY PROJECTS

Fiona Watt and Anna Rowley

Designed by Rebecca Halverson
Illustrated by Jonathan Woodcock

Photographs by Amanda Heywood • Calligraphy by Patricia Lovett
Edited by Felicity Brooks

Contents

Tips and reminders 50
Embossed notepaper 52
Cards and envelopes 54
A concertina birthday book 56
Giftwrap and tags 58
An interlocking gift box 60
Mugs and a bowl 62
Angel decoration and card 64
Decorating a terracotta pot 66
A sun clock 68
Calligraphy on a plate 70
An address book 72
A calligraphy nightshirt 74
A papier mâché bowl 76
Calligraphy and craft techniques 78
Index 80

Tips and reminders

The second part of this book contains a variety of exciting projects using calligraphy. These two pages will remind you of the different equipment you may need and also gives you some new techniques to try so that you can achieve successful results.

Equipment

Before you start any of the projects, check that you have all the things you will need. You will probably have some of the equipment, but you may need to go to a craft shop or a stationer's to buy one or two items.

Letter styles

On pages 40-41, you will find examples of different calligraphy alphabets. Some of the alphabets have small numbers around them which indicate the order in which you should make the pen strokes. The arrows show the direction of each stroke. Don't forget to lift your pen off the paper between every stroke.

Have a quick look at pages 9 and 78-79 for a reminder about how to space out letters and words evenly.

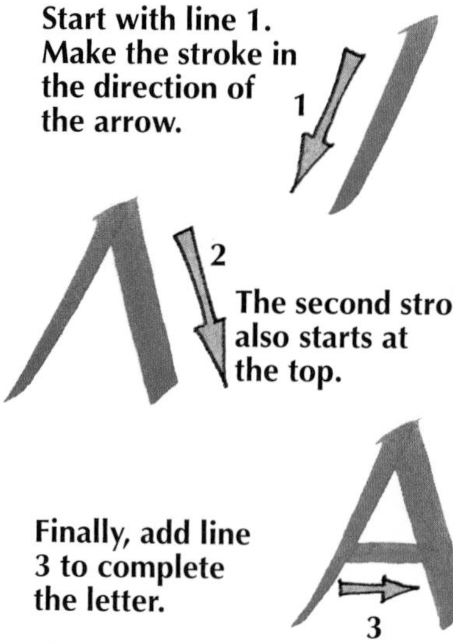

Start with line 1. Make the stroke in the direction of the arrow.
1
2
The second stroke also starts at the top.
Finally, add line 3 to complete the letter.
3

Pens and brushes

You will need a calligraphy pen for some of the projects. Felt-tipped calligraphy pens which are available in many stationery shops are the easiest to use and are suitable for most of the projects in this book. They have broad, square ends and come in a variety of widths and shades.

You can also a dip pen or a calligraphy fountain pen. They come with nibs of different widths and produce sharper lines than felt-tip pens. You will find information on pages 6-7 about how to use them.

Broad-edge brushes, also known as one-stroke brushes, can be bought from an art shop. There is more about them on page 28 and a brush alphabet on page 43.

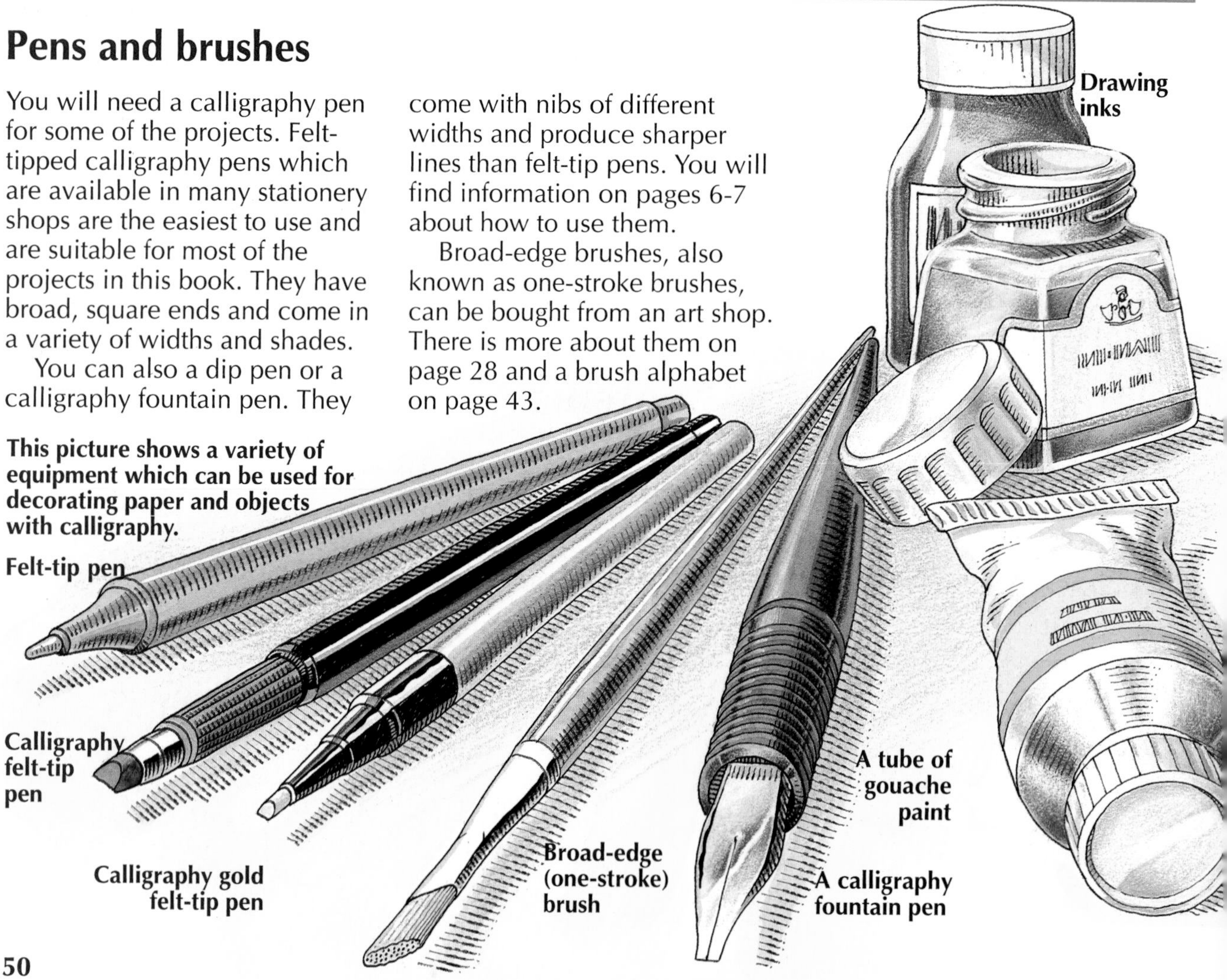

Drawing inks
Felt-tip pen
Calligraphy felt-tip pen
Calligraphy gold felt-tip pen
Broad-edge (one-stroke) brush
A tube of gouache paint
A calligraphy fountain pen

This picture shows a variety of equipment which can be used for decorating paper and objects with calligraphy.

Nib angles

When you write with a broad-edged nib the shape of the letter depends on the angle at which you hold the nib. Don't forget that for most alphabets, the nib should be held at the same angle throughout. The angle is shown by a diagram at the beginning of each alphabet (see pages 40-44).

90°

Angle of 90°

45°

Angle of 45°

30°

Angle of 30°

0°

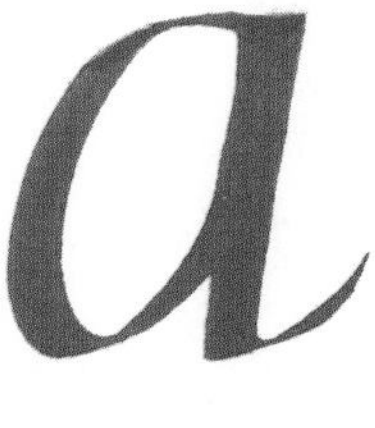

Nib horizontal

Double pencils

To get used to making smooth letter strokes with a calligraphy pen or brush, try taping two pencils together with masking tape. If you are right-handed, place the paper you are working on straight in front of you. If you are left-handed, you may find it easier to place the paper at an angle of about 45° on your work surface (see box below).

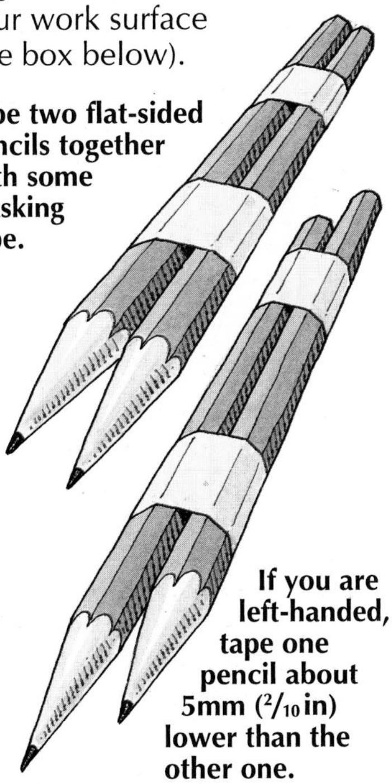

Tape two flat-sided pencils together with some masking tape.

If you are left-handed, tape one pencil about 5mm ($^2/_{10}$ in) lower than the other one.

Try making simple letter strokes with your double pencils.

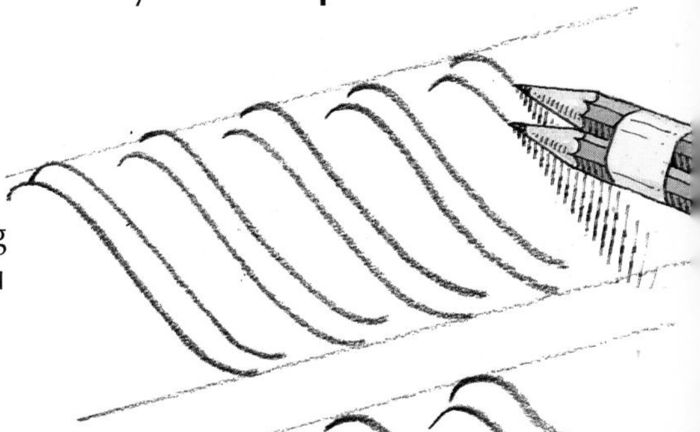

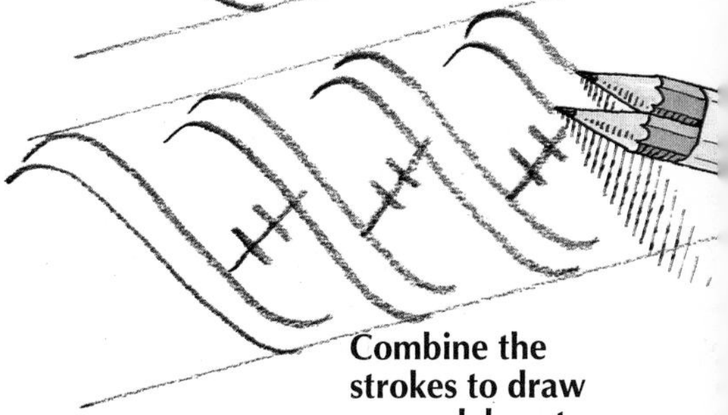

Combine the strokes to draw more elaborate patterns.

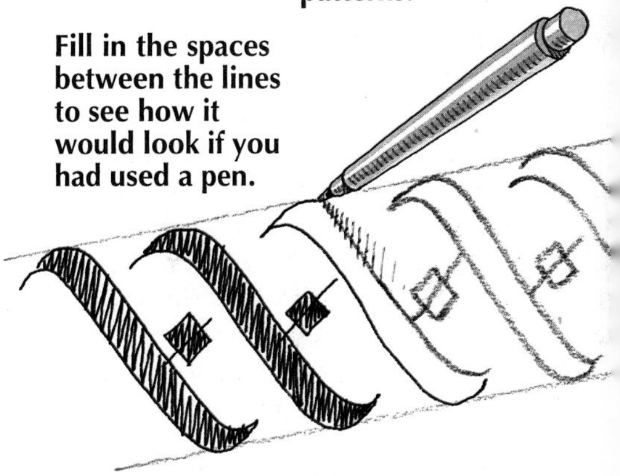

Fill in the spaces between the lines to see how it would look if you had used a pen.

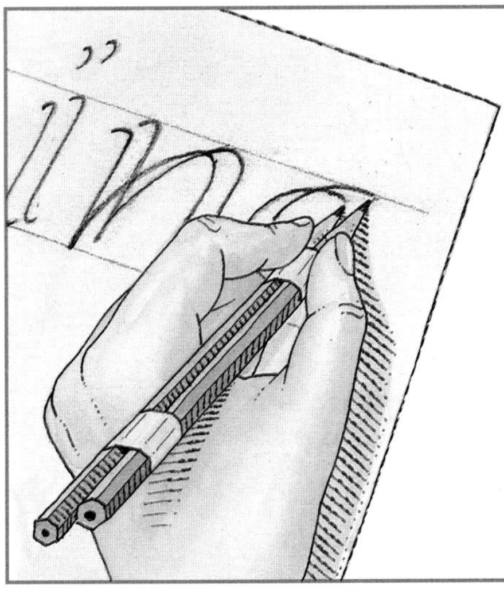

Left-handers

If you are left-handed, use a pen with a left-oblique nib or double pencils taped as shown above. You may need to change the angle of your wrist or the way you hold the pencils or pen, so that your wrist is under your lettering. Also, try placing your paper at an angle of 45° on your work surface.

Embossed notepaper

Embossing is the shaping or carving of letters or patterns so that they are raised above the surrounding surface.

You will need:

Writing paper and an envelope with a V-shaped flap
2 pieces of thin cardboard the same size as the writing paper
A craft knife
A teaspoon
Double pencils (see page 51)
Paper clips and glue
A fine felt-tip pen

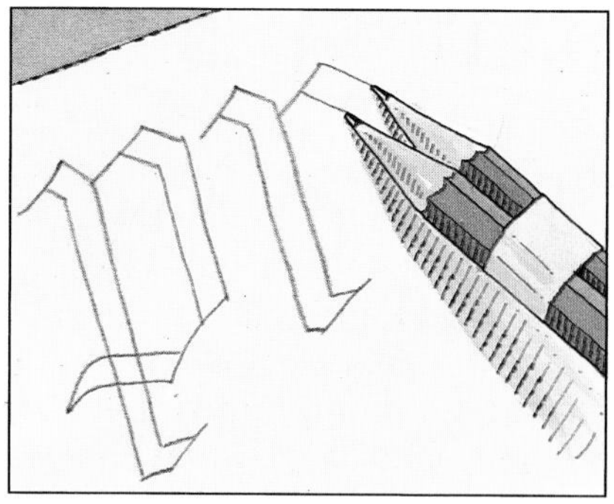

1. Using double pencils draw your initials on one piece of cardboard. Draw them in the same position as you want them to be on your writing paper.

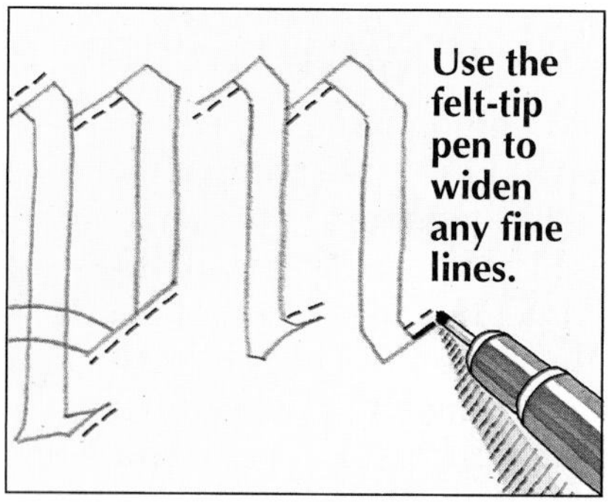
Use the felt-tip pen to widen any fine lines.

2. Make any thin parts of letters about 2mm ($^{1}/_{16}$in) wide, then put some old magazines under the cardboard to protect your work surface.

Keep any cut-out middle pieces of letters.

3. Cut out each letter with the craft knife. Then turn the cardboard over and glue it onto the other piece of cardboard. Glue any middle pieces in place.

4. Place a sheet of writing paper over the cardboard. Secure it in place with some paper clips. Lay the paper and cardboard on a flat surface.

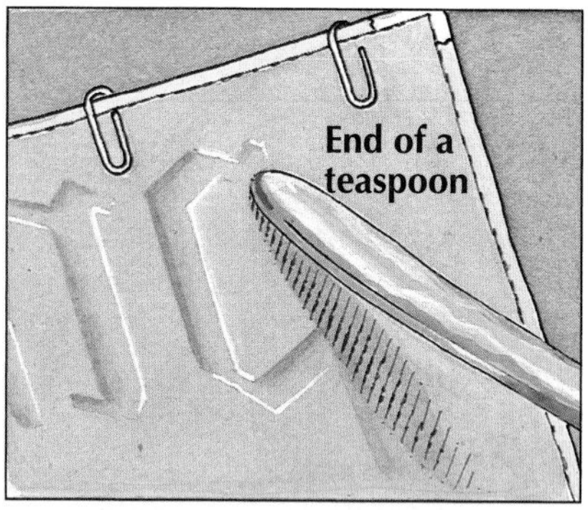
End of a teaspoon

5. Gently push the paper into the cut-out letters, using the end of the spoon. Push right into the edges of the letters to make crisp lines.

6. Carefully remove the paper clips and turn the paper over. You can make many sheets of embossed paper using the same cardboard cut-out.

Embossing an envelope

Use paper clips to attach an envelope to your cardboard cut-out. Make sure that your initials will be the right way up when the envelope is sealed. Use the teaspoon to smooth the flap into the cut-out letters as you did for the writing paper.

You could emboss your initials on the cover of a small book. (See pages 72-73 for instructions on how to make a book.)

Patterns

As well as letters, you can also emboss patterns. Use simple shapes as they are easiest to cut out.

Cards and envelopes

You will need:

Thick, bright paper
Calligraphy pens
Tracing paper
Scissors and a craft knife
Glue
A ruler
Parcel ribbon

The pattern on the tied card was drawn with a pen and gouache paint (available from an art suppliers).

The hearts on the tree card were drawn with a calligraphy pen.

The lines on the striped, zigzag card were painted in ink using a homemade felt-tip pen (see page 59).

HAPPY EASTER
BUONA PASCUA
VROLIJK PASEN
GROSSES BIS
WITH LOV
TANTI BAC

Tree card

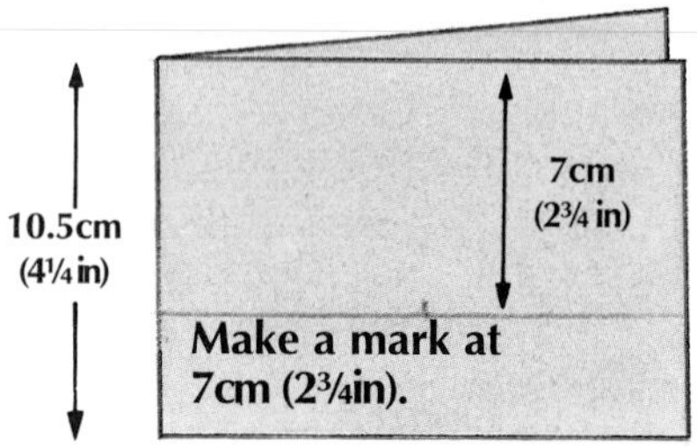

10.5cm (4¼in)
7cm (2¾in)
Make a mark at 7cm (2¾in).

1. Cut a piece of paper that measures 10.5 x 28cm (4¼ x 11in). Fold it in half. Draw a faint line 7cm (2¾in) from the top.

To transfer your lettering to the card (see page 78).

2. On tracing paper, draw around the front and draw in the faint line. Write your message along the line and on the pot and trunk.

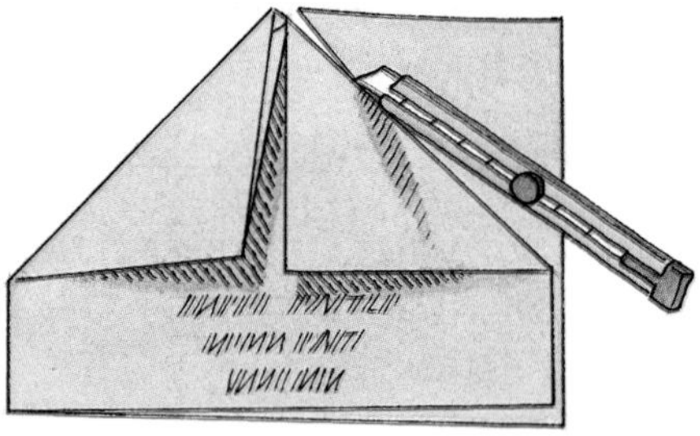

3. Fold the top two corners in so they meet in the middle at the mark on the line. Cut off the top layer of the right-hand flap.

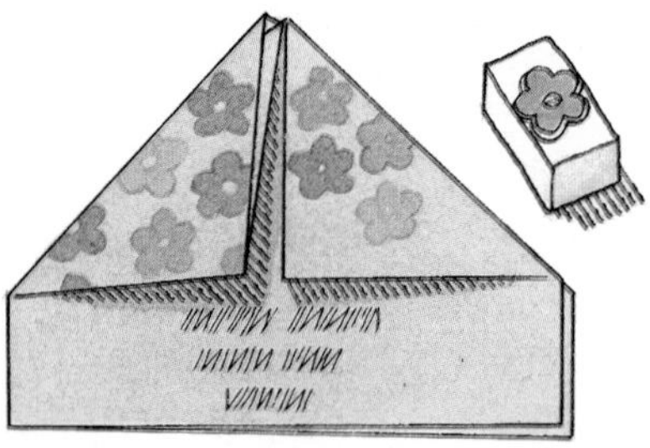

4. You could use a calligraphy pen to draw a pattern on the flaps, or print a design with a rubber stamp (see pages 58-59).

Zigzag card

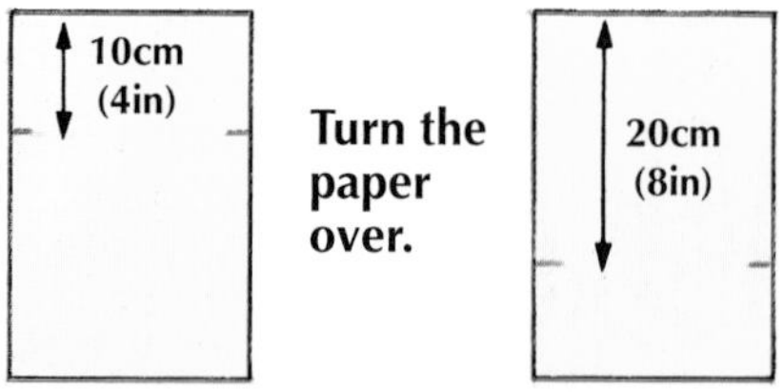

10cm (4in)
Turn the paper over.
20cm (8in)

1. Cut a piece of paper 20 x 30cm (8 x 12in). Make pencil marks at 10cm (4in) on one side and 20cm (8in) on the other side.

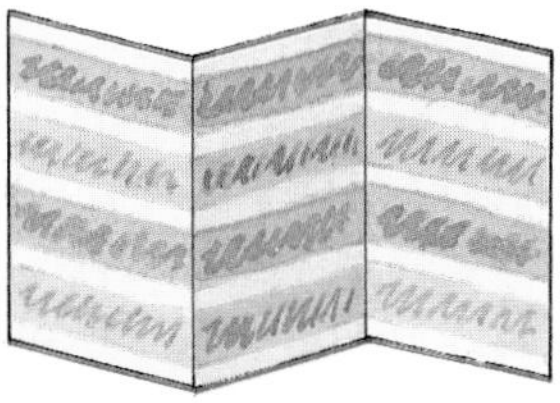

Decorate the front and write your message on the back.

2. Lightly score the paper along the marks you have made. Fold it first one way and then the other to make a zigzag.

Tied card

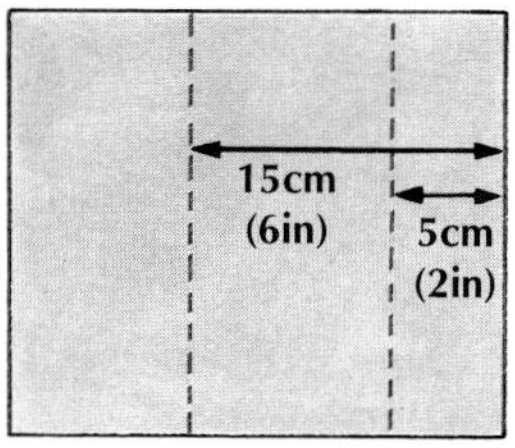
15cm
(6in)
5cm
(2in)

1. Cut a piece of bright paper 24 x 20cm (9½ x 8in). Mark and score lines 5cm (2in) and 15cm (6in) from the right-hand side.

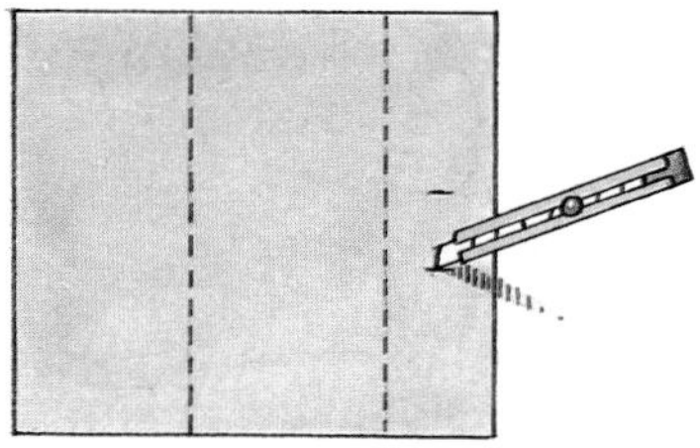

2. Use a craft knife to make two slits, 1cm (½ in) long on the narrow section, 8cm (3in) in from each end.

Open out the paper.

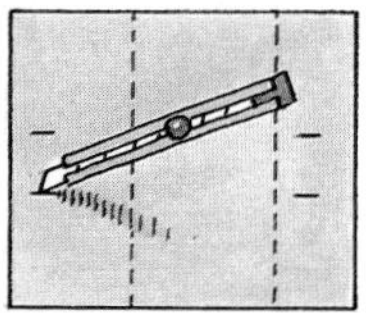

Cut along the scored slits.

3. Fold in the flaps, with the narrow one on top. Slide the craft knife through each slit to score lines on the layer below.

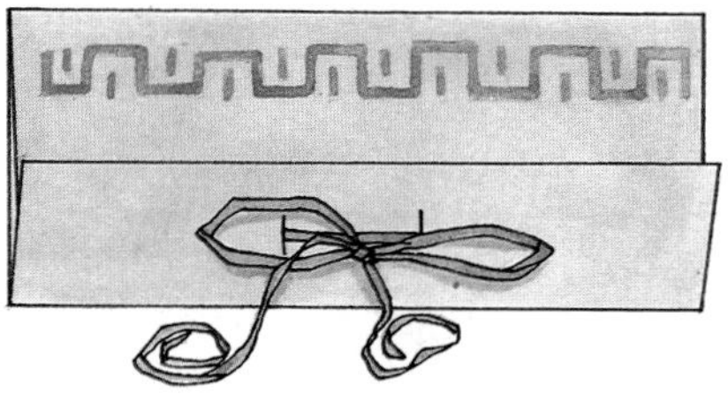

4. Decorate the front and the inside of the card. Thread a piece of parcel ribbon through both sets of slits and tie a bow.

Envelopes

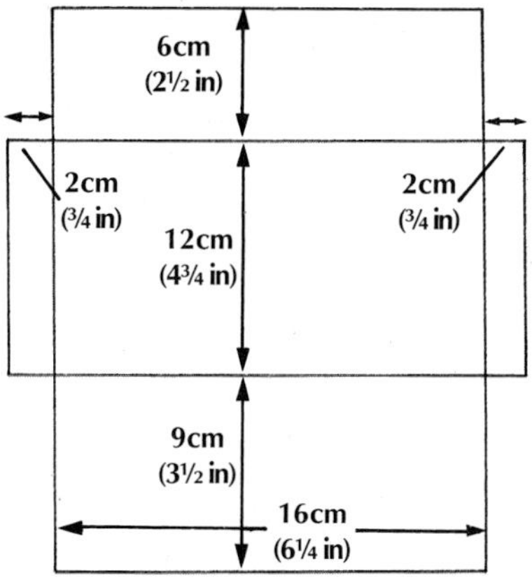
6cm
(2½ in)
2cm
(¾ in)
12cm
(4¾ in)
2cm
(¾ in)
9cm
(3½ in)
16cm
(6¼ in)

The tree card will fit in this size.

1. Copy the measurements above onto paper using a ruler and pencil. If you want to make an envelope for the other cards, change the width of the large rectangle from 16cm (6¼in) to 21cm (8½in).

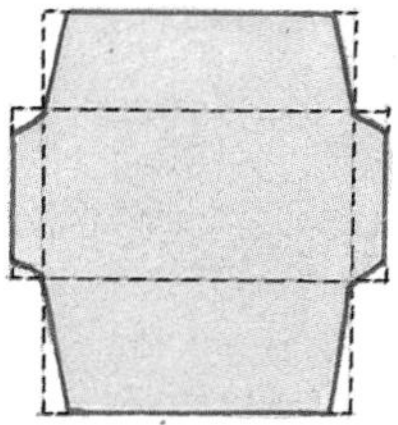

Cut around the outline shown in red.

2. Mark points 1cm (½in) from each corner. Join these points to the corners of the middle rectangle.

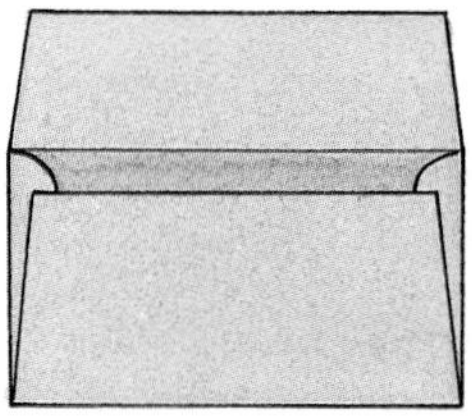

To seal the envelope, stick the top flap with a little glue.

3. Score lightly along each line and fold in the sides. Fold up the bottom. Stick this to the sides with some glue.

A concertina birthday book

You will need:

2 pieces of stiff cardboard
10 x 17cm (4 x 6¾in)
A sheet of paper 56 x 15cm
(22 x 6in) for the pages
2 pieces of giftwrap 14 x 21cm
(5½ x 8½ in)
4 pieces of 25cm (10in) ribbon
A glue stick
A calligraphy pen
A ruler and a craft knife

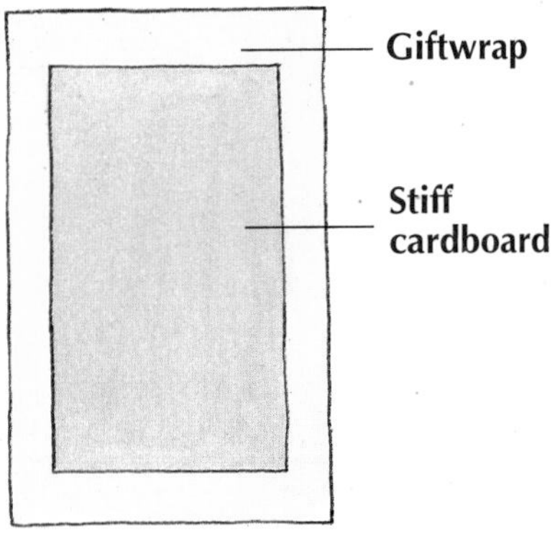
Giftwrap
Stiff cardboard

1. To make the two covers, cut the cardboard and giftwrap to the correct sizes, using a craft knife and ruler. Glue the cardboard in the middle of the giftwrap, leaving equal margins all around.

MAART

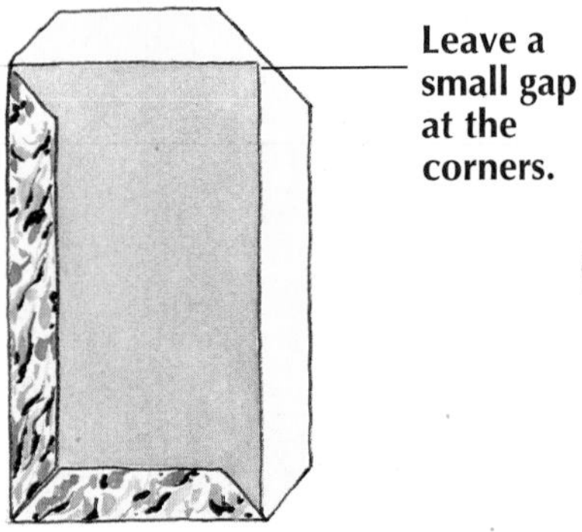
Leave a small gap at the corners.

2. Use scissors to trim the corners off the giftwrap, close to, but not touching the corners of the cardboard. Fold the giftwrap over the edges and glue them down carefully.

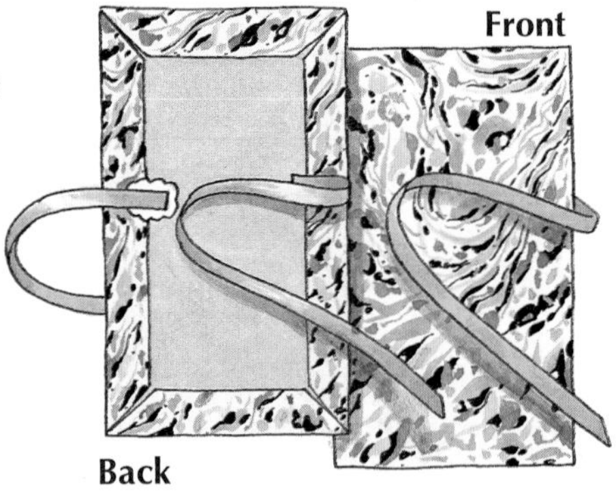
Front
Back

3. Use glue to stick the ribbons onto the inside of each cover. Make sure there is an equal amount of ribbon at each side. Trim each end diagonally to stop the ribbons from fraying.

Fold the paper into a concertina.

4. Make faint pencil marks every 8cm (3in) at the top and bottom edges of the long strip of paper. Neatly score and fold the paper one way and then the other at each set of marks (see page 79).

MAYO
JUNI
MAGGIO
JUNIO

You could decorate the covers with lettering or embossing (see pages 52-53), rather than using giftwrap.

Lettering Styles

You could use a single large letter instead of the whole word for each month. Decorate the inside of the letter with ink or paint in a contrasting shade.

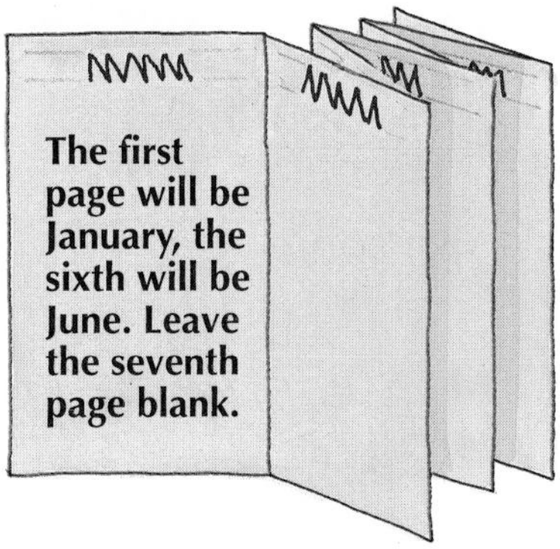

The first page will be January, the sixth will be June. Leave the seventh page blank.

5. Rule double lines along the top for the name of each month. The distance between the lines depends on the size of your nib (see page 78). Write the names of the months between the lines.

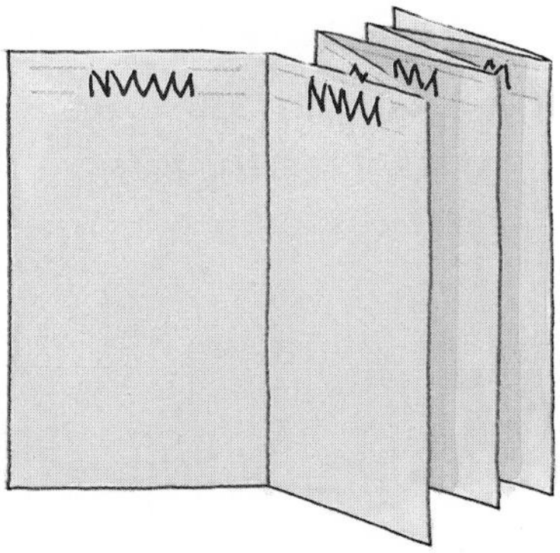

6. Measure out the same lines on the other side. The lettering for July will be on page 8 and so on. December will be on page 13. Leave page 14 blank as this will be stuck to a cover.

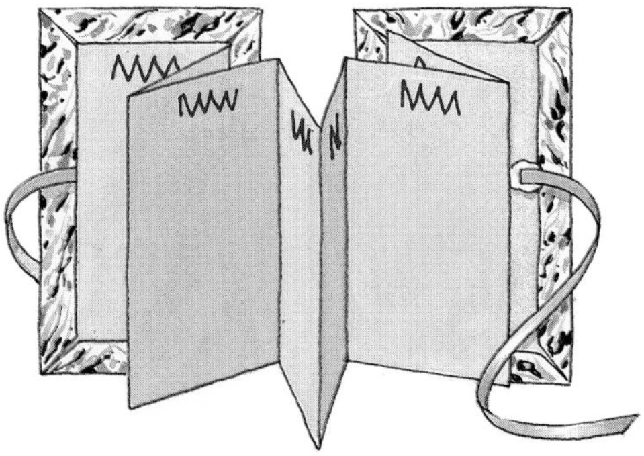

7. When you have finished lettering both sides, use glue to stick page 14 in the middle of the front cover. Glue page 7 onto the back cover. Tie the ribbons to close the book.

Giftwrap and tags

You can use calligraphy to decorate large sheets of paper, such as brown parcel paper. You could also experiment with giftwrap that has a simple pattern on it. Before you start, calculate roughly how much paper you will need to wrap your present.

Gold ink used with a homemade pen (see right)

Brown parcel paper printed with a rubber stamp

Use some of your giftwrap to make a matching tag.

Stripes drawn with a felt-tip pen and a cotton-tipped stick, then printed with a rubber stamp

Rubber stamps

You will need:

A large eraser
A craft knife
Tracing paper
A soft and a hard pencil
Double pencils (see page 51) or a calligraphy pen
A large sheet of paper
An ink pad from a stationer's

1. Draw around the eraser onto the tracing paper. Draw a letter or shape inside the outline, using the pencils or a pen.

2. Turn the tracing paper over, place it on the eraser. Use a hard pencil to transfer the lettering to the eraser (see page 78).

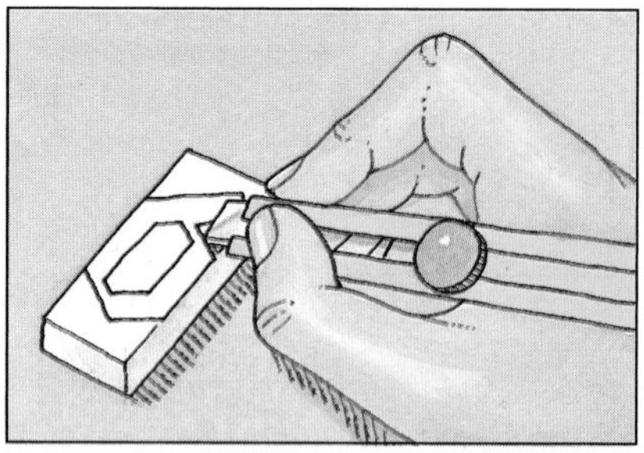

3. Put the eraser on a cutting surface (see page 79). Carefully cut around the outline of the letter or shape using a craft knife.

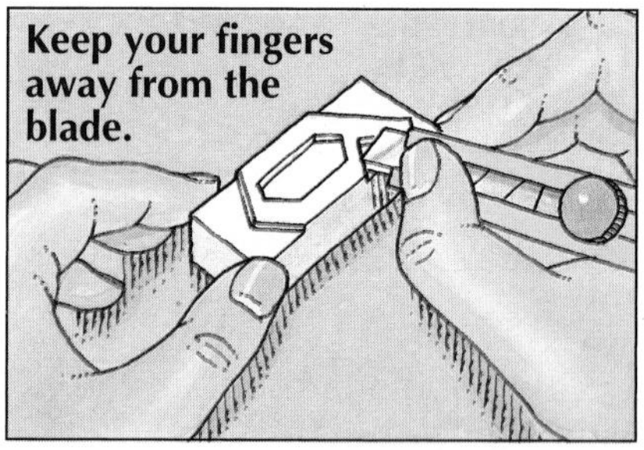

Keep your fingers away from the blade.

4. Carefully slice away the area around the letter, so that the letter stands about 2mm ($^{1}/_{16}$in) above the surface of the eraser.

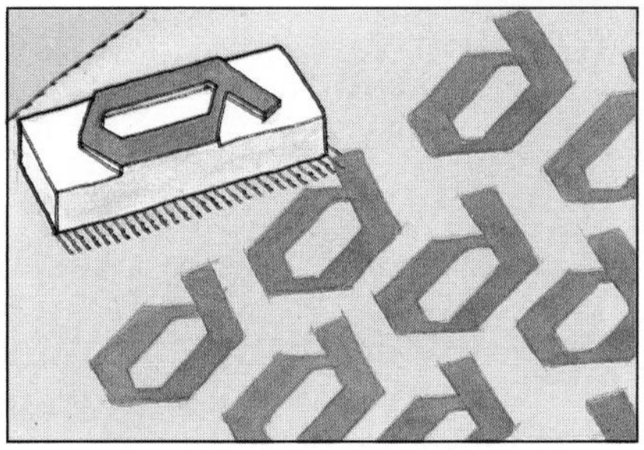

5. Press the rubber stamp onto the ink pad. Try out various repeated patterns before printing onto your large piece of paper.

Fluid writing

Another technique is to use artists' masking fluid from an art supplier's, with a homemade pen (see right).

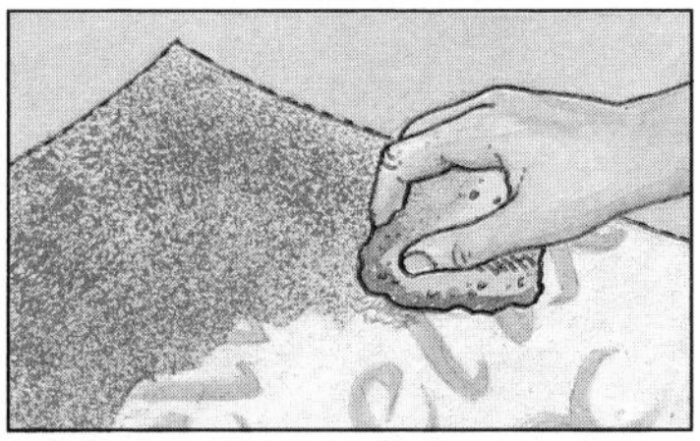

Paint the fluid onto paper. When it is dry, sponge ink over it and leave it to dry.

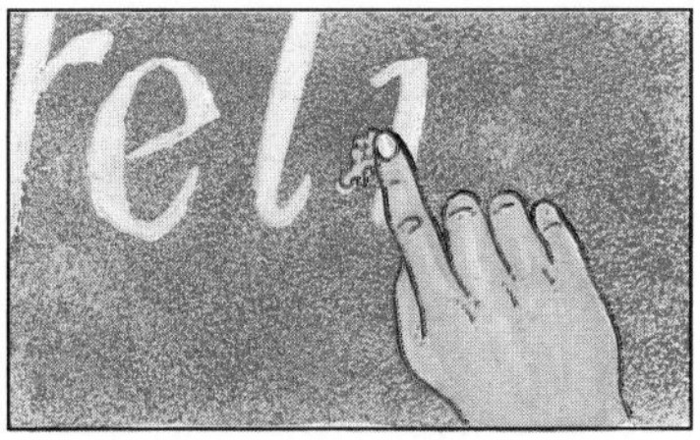

Gently rub the surface of the masking fluid with your finger or an eraser to reveal your lettering.

Homemade pens

You will need:

A craft knife
Thick cardboard
Plastic food wrap
Felt
A rubber band
2 cotton-tipped sticks
Ink or paint

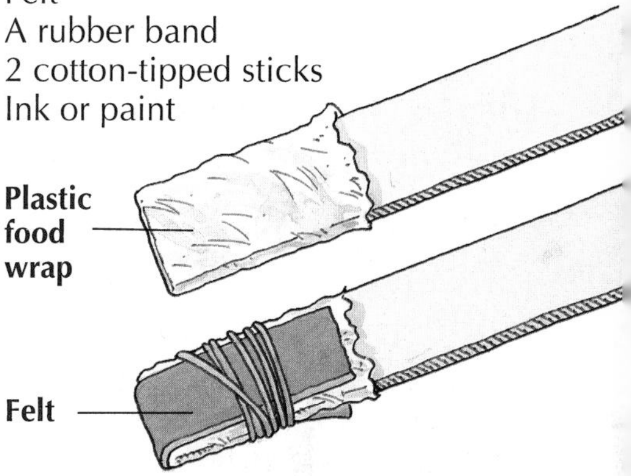

Cut the cardboard into a strip 15 x 2cm (6 x ¾in). Wrap some food wrap around one end of it. Cut a strip of felt the same width as the cardboard. Secure it over the end of the cardboard with a rubber band. Dip the pen into ink or paint and write with it. For smaller letters, cut a narrower strip.

You can also make a double-nibbed pen using the same method. Once you have secured the food wrap and the felt, cut a V-shape into the end of the pen, through the layers.

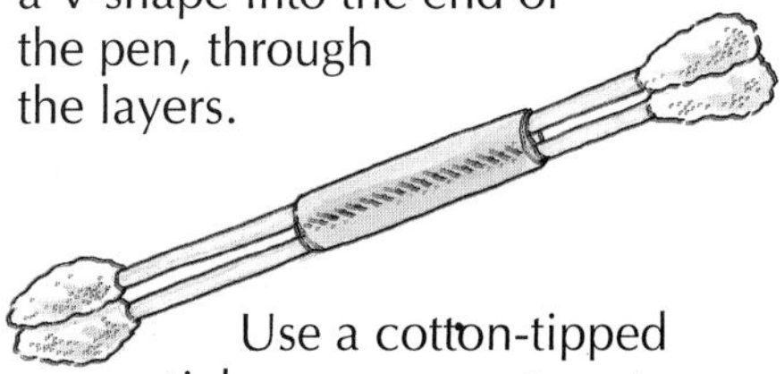

Use a cotton-tipped stick as a pen, or tape two together to make a thicker pen. Try using this with ink instead of using a felt-tip pen.

An interlocking gift box

You will need:

2 sheets of cardboard, about the thickness of a cereal box, in contrasting shades
A craft knife and scissors
Glue
Tracing paper
Calligraphy pen or a broad-edge brush and paint
A ruler
An eraser

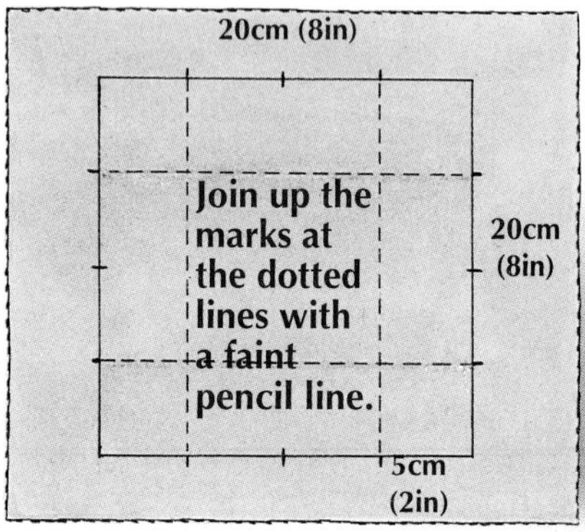

1. To make a box measuring 10 x10cm (4 x 4in), start by drawing a 20 x 20cm (8 x 8in) square on both pieces of cardboard. Measure and mark points lightly in pencil every 5cm (2in) along each side.

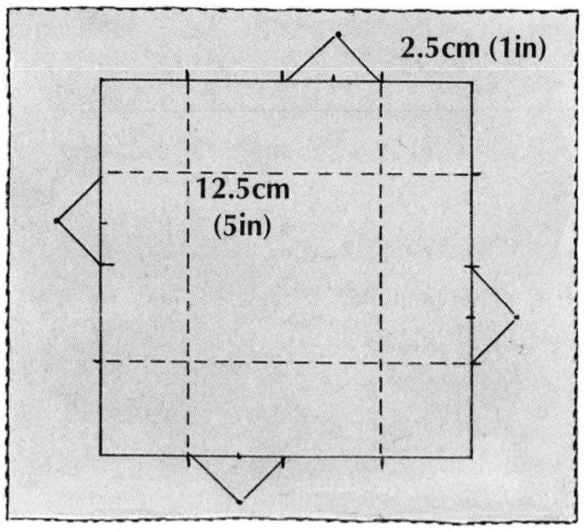

2. Mark 12.5cm (5in) along each side on both squares. Draw a dot 2.5cm (1in) above each of these marks. Join each dot to the marks on the square either side of it.

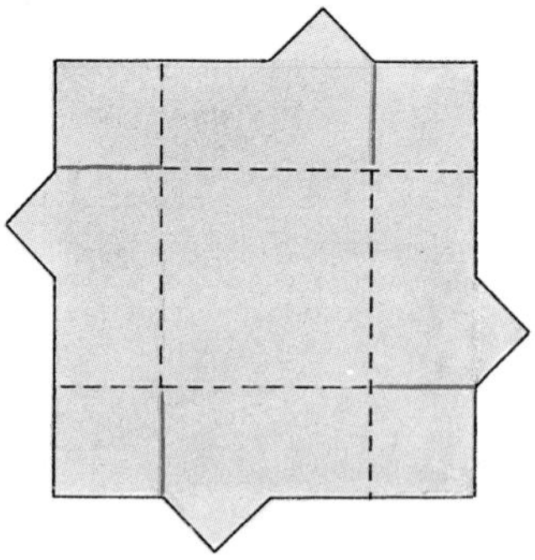

3. Using a craft knife and a ruler, carefully cut out the two halves of the box along the outlines. Also cut along the red lines indicated in the picture.

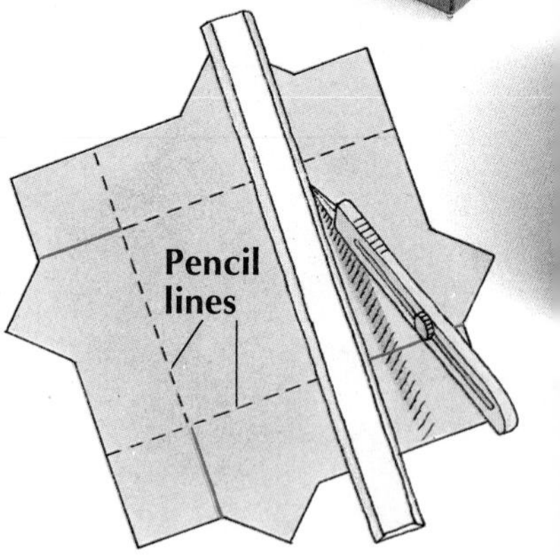

4. Gently score along all the dotted lines shown above with a craft knife (see page 79). Remove all your pencil lines from each box with an eraser.

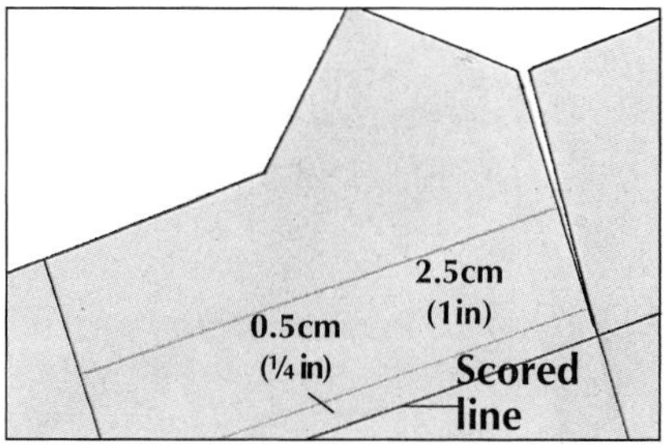
2.5cm
(1in)
0.5cm
(¼in)
Scored
line

5. Decorate your box before you stick it together. Draw two faint pencil lines 0.5cm (¼in) and 2.5cm (1in) from the scored lines, as guidelines for the letters.

To make a box with wavy edges, open a pair of compasses to 2.5cm (1in) and draw a semicircle at the 12.5cm (5in) mark (see stage 2).

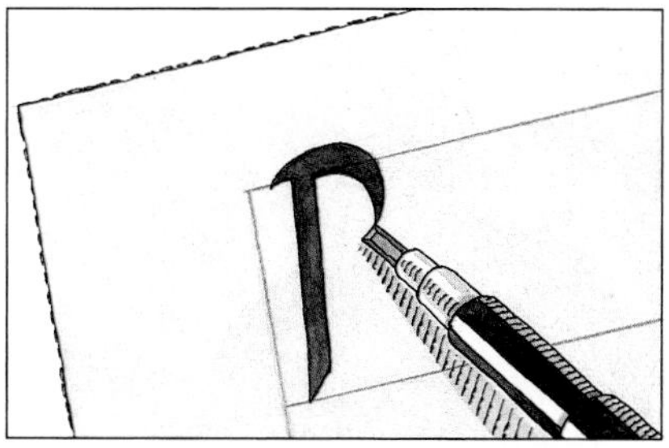

6. Trace over the guidelines onto a piece of tracing paper. Use the guidelines to help with the sizing and spacing of your lettering (see page 78).

7. Transfer the lettering to the side or top of the lid (see page 78). Use either a pen or a broad-edge brush and paint for the lettering.

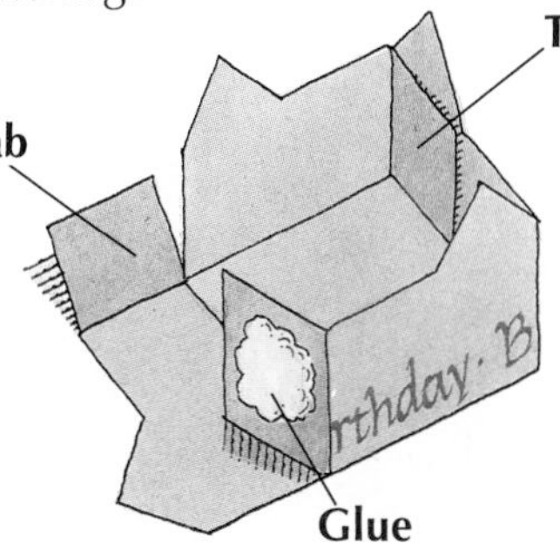
Tab
Tab
Glue

8. Fold up the edges and bend each tab at right angles to the fold. Glue the tabs inside.

9. Finally, interlock the two halves, making sure that all the triangles are on the outside.

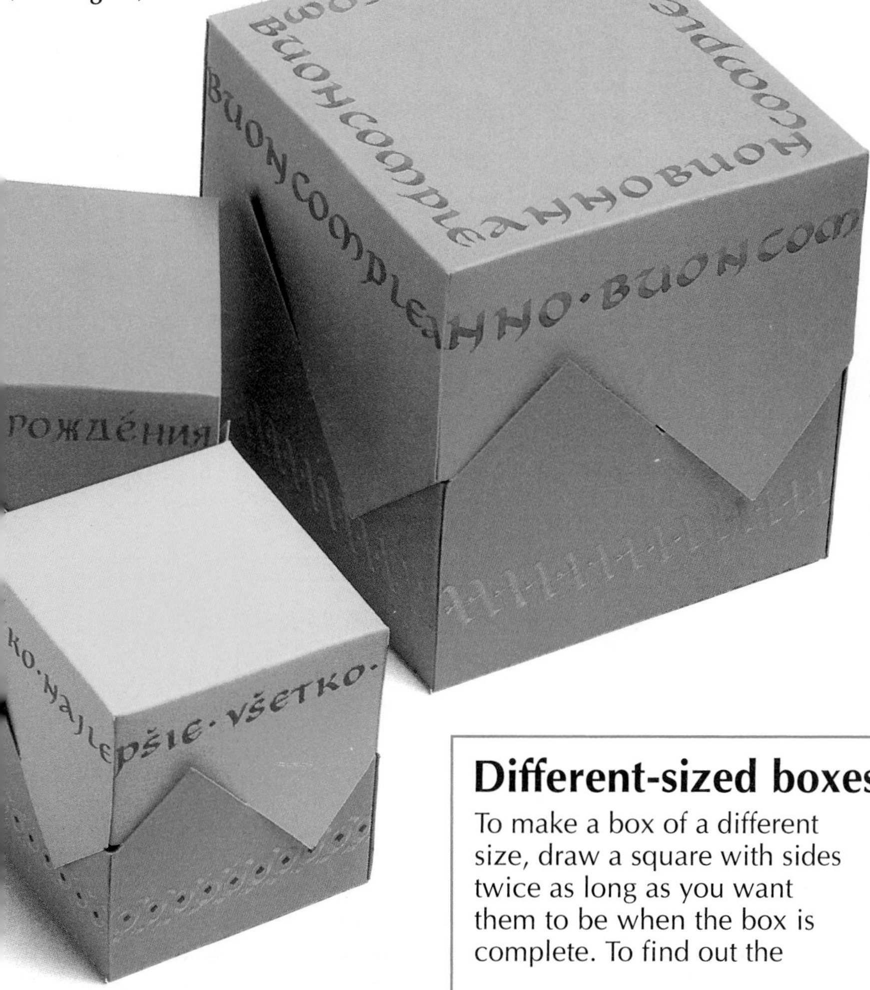

Different-sized boxes

To make a box of a different size, draw a square with sides twice as long as you want them to be when the box is complete. To find out the distance between the marks in step 1, divide the length of the side by four. The height of the points in step 2 is half the distance between these marks.

Mugs and a bowl

You will need :

A plain china mug
Ceramic paint which hardens in an oven (available in craft shops)
Tracing paper
Clear book-covering film
A craft knife and scissors
An old toothbrush
Double pencils (see page 51)
Paper towels
A ballpoint pen
A small, clean plastic container
Old newspapers
A black felt-tip pen
Masking tape

You could save the letters you cut out at step 4 and use them to decorate a matching plate (see pages 70-71).

Remember to harden the paint on your finished object by following the paint maker's instructions.

Add simple decorations, such as dots or flowers between the letters.

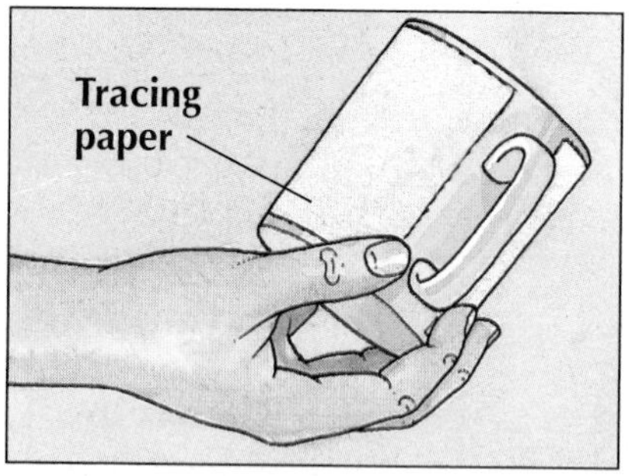

1. Cut a strip of tracing paper about the same height as your mug and long enough to fit around it.

Make the thinnest part of the letters 3mm ($^1/_8$in) wide.

2. Using double pencils, write a message or a name to fit on the tracing paper. Outline the letters with a black felt-tip pen.

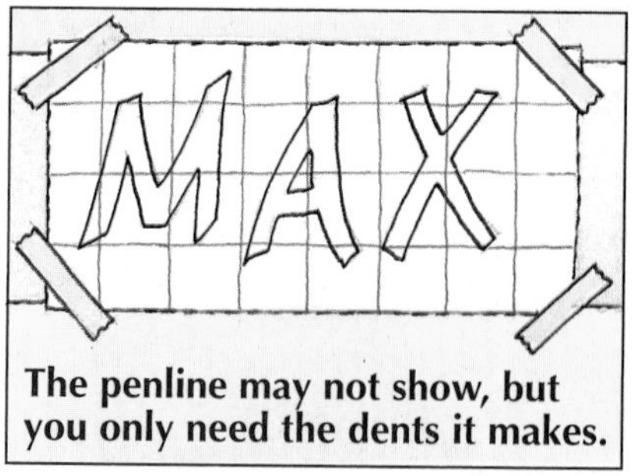

The penline may not show, but you only need the dents it makes.

3. Cut some film to fit over the tracing paper. Tape it, shiny side upward, over the letters. Trace around them with a ballpoint pen.

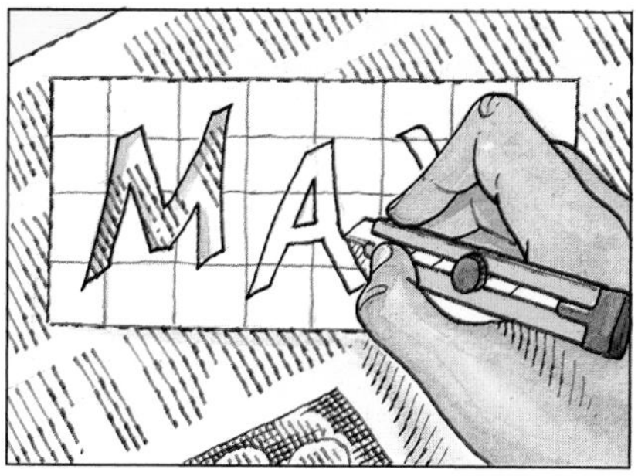

4. Place the film on a cutting surface. Use a craft knife to cut out the letters. Keep any middle pieces from the letters as you will need to stick them on the mug.

Stick in any middle pieces.
Cut-out area
Film

5. It is easier to stick the film onto the mug if you cut the film into smaller pieces before peeling off the backing paper. Be careful not to cut the letters.

6. Completely cover the rest of the mug, including the handle with pieces of tape. Put lots of paper towels inside the mug so that it is kept clean.

7. In the plastic container, mix a little ceramic paint with water until it is like thin cream. Cover an area with newspaper and put your mug in the middle of it.

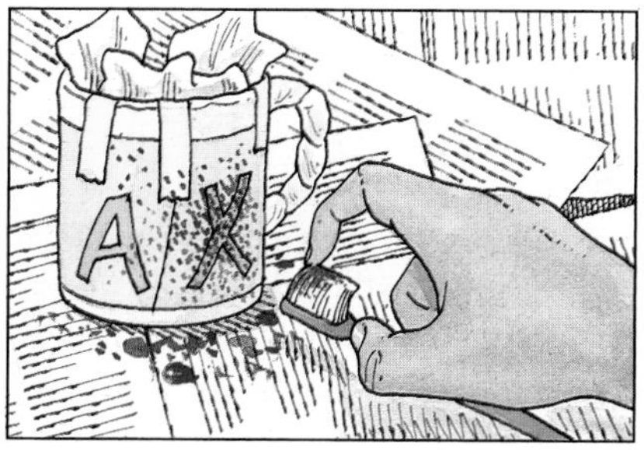

8. To spray the letters, dip the toothbrush into the paint and hold it near the mug. Flick your fingernail along the bristles until the letter spaces are covered.

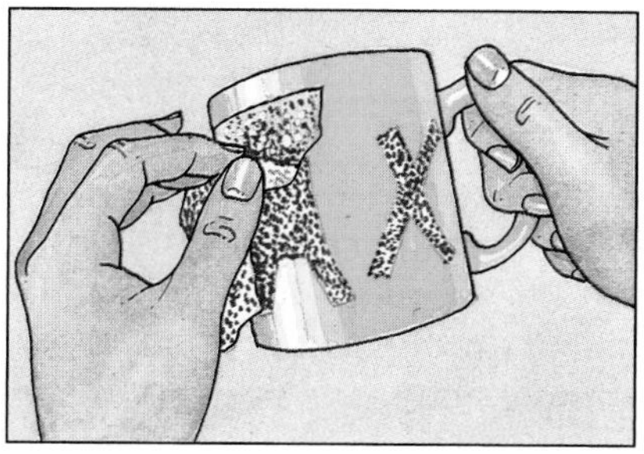

9. You could add another shade of paint once the first has dried. When all the paint is dry, peel off the film. Follow the maker's instructions to harden the paint.

Decorating a bowl

You can use exactly the same technique to decorate the outside of a bowl. To calculate the length of your message, cut a strip of tracing paper long enough to fit around the outside of the bowl.

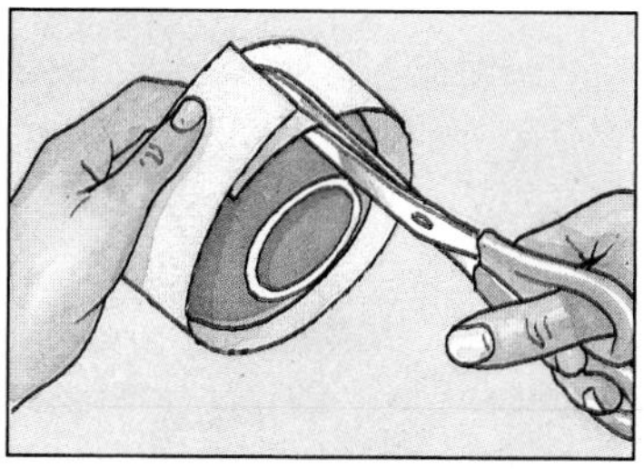

More mugs

Buy a mug with stripes on it. Draw parallel lines, the same width as the stripes. Draw a pattern between the lines then trace it onto the film.

Draw a simple calligraphy pattern (see page 67) and spray it around the base of the mug. Add small dots in a different shade with a fine paintbrush.

Buy a mug with a simple design on it. Trace the shapes onto tracing paper and add letters to fill the spaces. Try putting the letters at at different angles.

Angel decorations and cards

You will need:

Thick white paper 25 x 25cm (10 x 10in)
A pair of compasses
A pencil and a ruler
Calligraphy pens
A small piece of gold paper
Tracing paper
A needle and thread
A craft knife and scissors

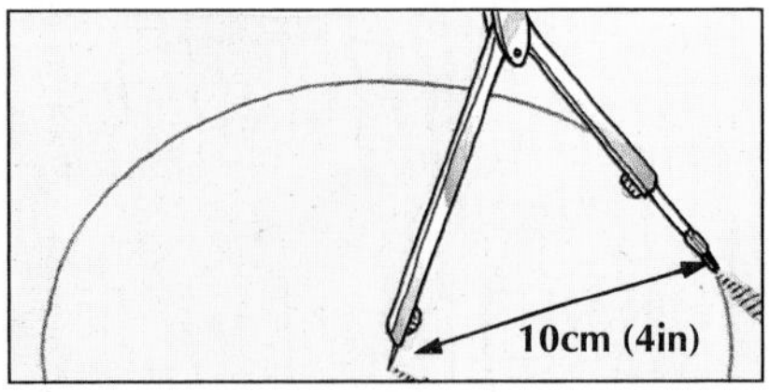
10cm (4in)

1. Open your compasses to 10cm (4in) and draw a circle on the white paper. The diameter of your circle should be 20cm (8in).

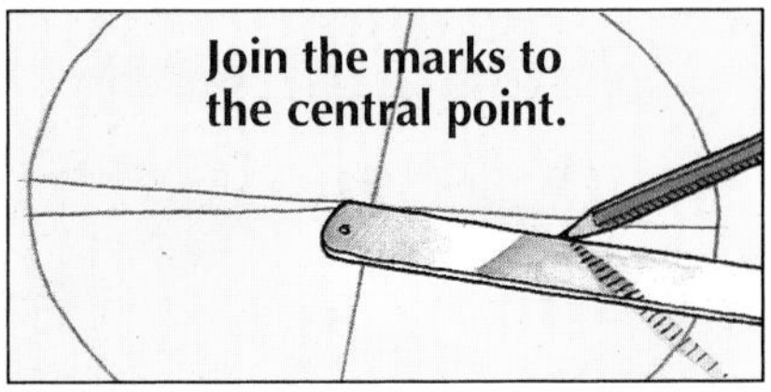
Join the marks to the central point.

2. Divide the circle into quarters with faint lines. Mark points on the outside of the circle 8mm ($^3/_8$in) below the horizontal line.

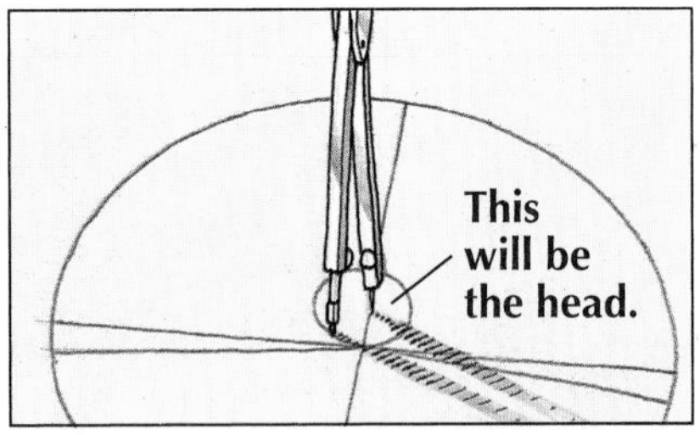
This will be the head.

3. Open the compasses to 1.5cm ($^5/_8$in). Starting with the pencil lead on the central point, draw a circle above the horizontal line.

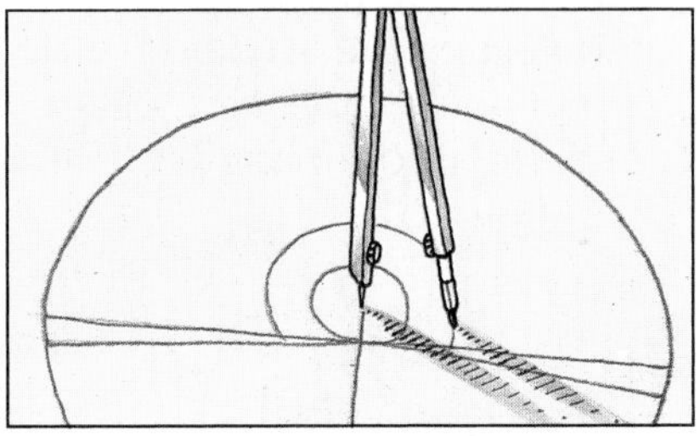

4. Open the compasses to 3cm ($1^1/_8$in) and with the point in the same place, draw an arc between the two sloping lines.

You could make several angels and hang them from different lengths of thread.

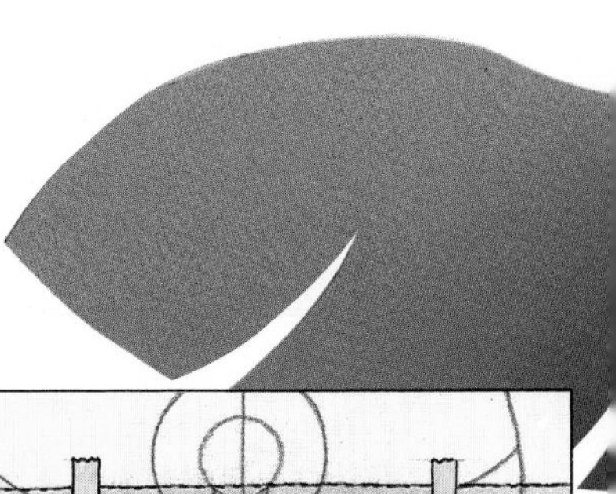

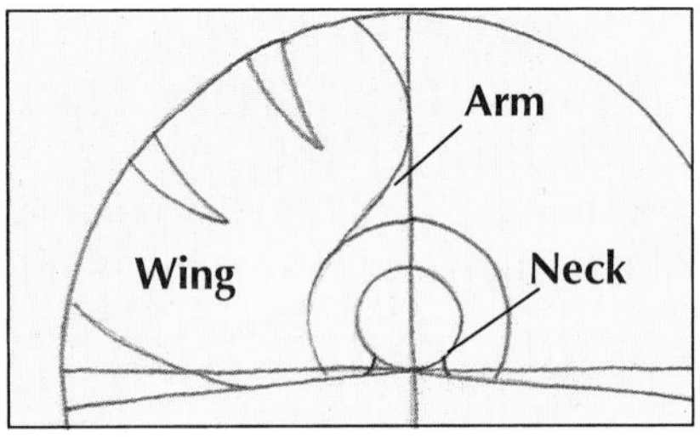
Arm
Wing
Neck

5. Draw the shapes for the wings, neck and arms on one side of the circle as shown on the diagram above.

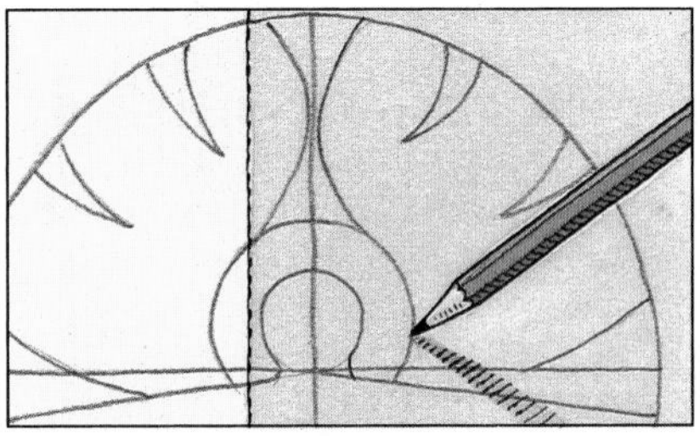

6. Trace around the shapes, turn the paper over and transfer the shapes to the other side of the circle (see page 78).

Transfer the lettering onto the angel.
Buon Natale

7. Trace around the skirt. Write a message which fits in the middle 6cm ($2^1/_2$in) of the skirt, so it can be read when the angel is folded.

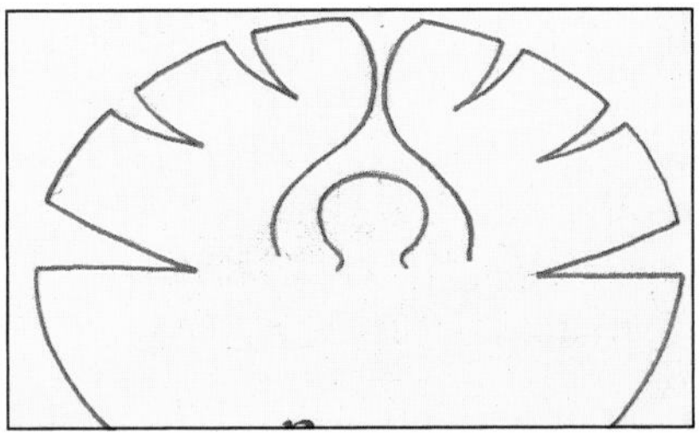

8. Cut along all the lines shown in red with a craft knife or scissors. Remove all the pencil lines with an eraser.

Assembling the angel

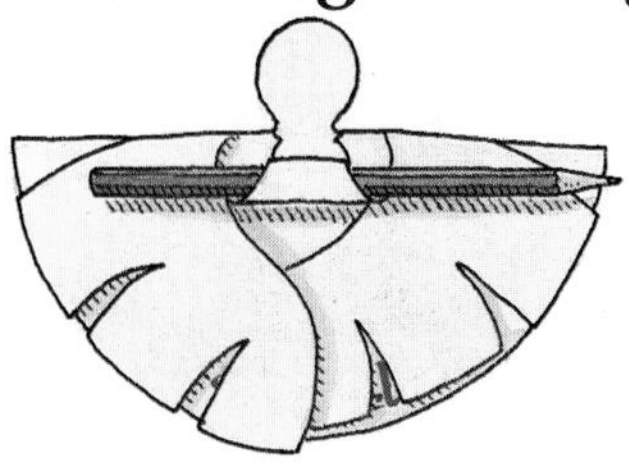

Fold the wings and the arms forward and roll the arms around a pencil to curl them.

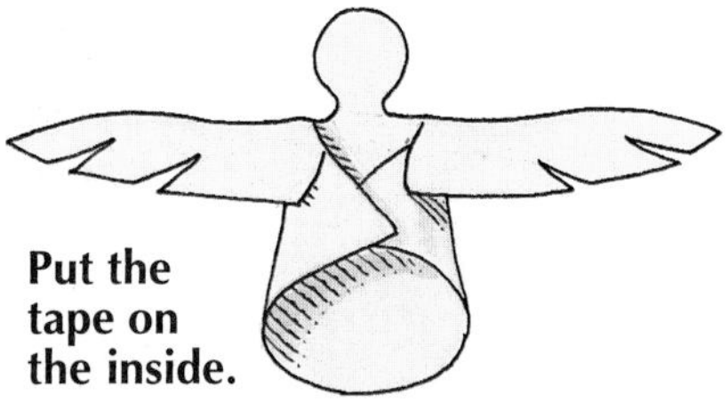
Put the tape on the inside.

Bend the skirt of the angel around to make a cone shape and stick it together with tape.

Buon Natale
Happy Christmas
Prettige Kerstdagen

The angel as a card

To use the angel as a Christmas card, follow steps 1 to 8. Don't forget to include a halo. Either buy an envelope at least 21 x 21cm (8½ x 8½in) to fit the card, or make one following the instructions on page 55, adjusting the measurements so that the middle rectangle becomes a square measuring 21 x 21cm (8½ x 8½in) and the right one measures 21 x 18cm (8½ x 7in).

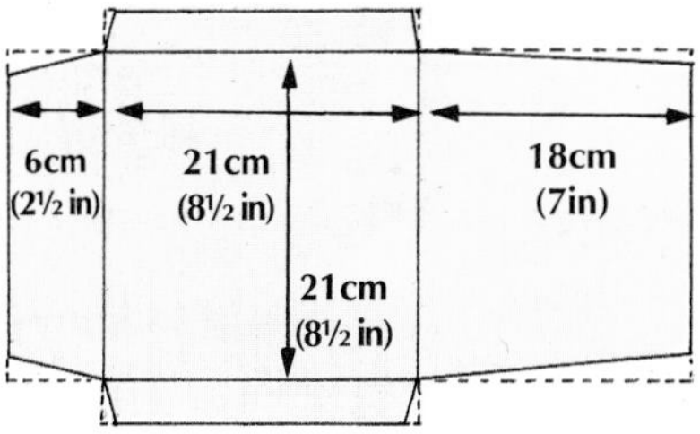
6cm (2½ in)
21cm (8½ in)
18cm (7in)
21cm (8½ in)

Copy the instructions from the box (below left) on how to assemble the angel. Send them in the envelope with your card.

Buon Natale

Draw a small circle with a tab on gold paper for the halo. Stick it onto the angel's head.

To make a hanging decoration, push a needle with thread through the top of the angel's head and tie the ends to make a loop.

Decorating a terracotta pot

You will need:

A clean terracotta plant pot
Tracing paper and masking tape
A broad-edge (one-stroke) paint brush from an art supplier's
Artist's acrylic paints
A plastic lid
Carbon paper (see page 78)
Double pencils (see page 51)
Scrap paper

Instead of drawing a pattern, you could write a name around the pot, or combine lettering and patterns.

Leave your pot on a pile of old newspapers to dry out.

1. Make sure the surface of the terracotta pot is absolutely clean. If you need to wash it, leave it overnight to dry out as this type of pot absorbs a lot of water.

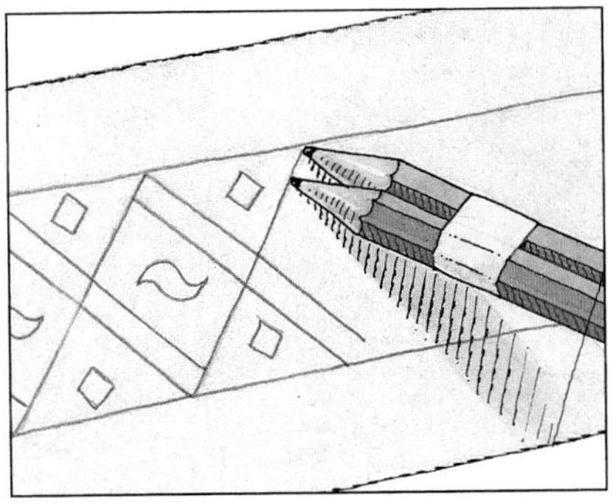

2. To calculate the length of your decoration, cut a strip of tracing paper which fits around your pot. On scrap paper, try out different patterns using double pencils or copy some from below.

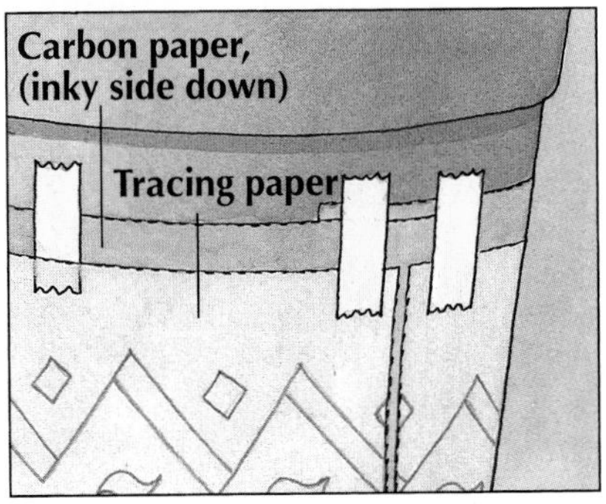
Carbon paper, (inky side down)
Tracing paper

3. Once you are happy with your design, trace it onto the strip of tracing paper. Stick a piece of carbon paper onto the pot, inky side down, then tape the tracing paper over it.

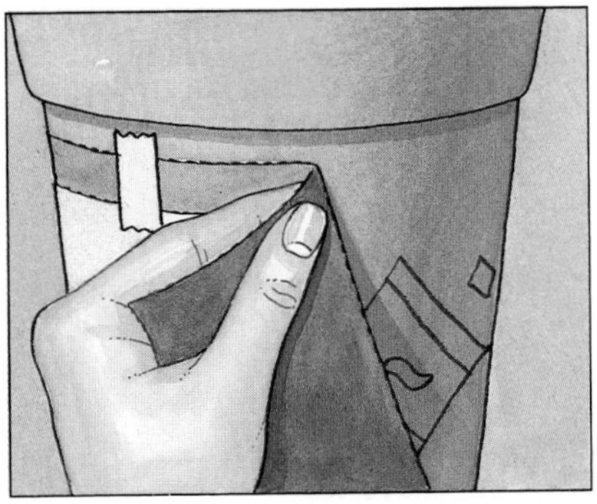

4. Use a pencil with a hard lead to trace over the outline of your pattern (see page 78). Check that it has traced completely before pulling off the papers.

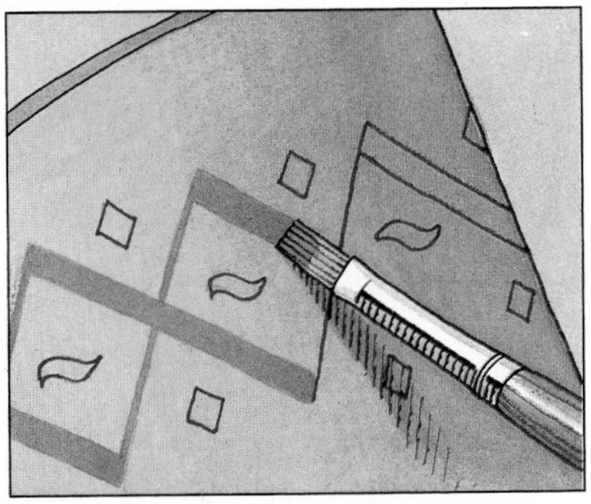

5. On a lid, mix some acrylic paint with water so that it is like thin cream. Paint over the pattern with the brush. Some shades may need two coats of paint.

Depending on the shape of your pot, you could paint your decoration or lettering around the rim or the base of the pot, or both.

Calligraphic patterns

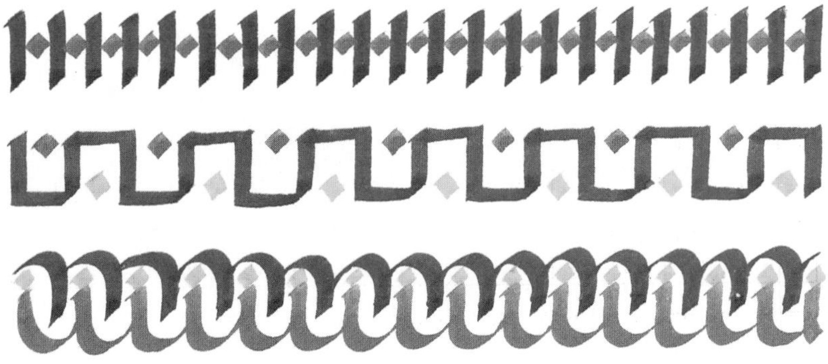

A sun clock

This clock could be hung on a wall by attaching some string to the back with masking tape.

When Roman numerals are used for the numbers on a clockface, number 4 is often shown as IIII, rather than IV. This is to balance with VIII on the opposite side.

You will need:

A clock mechanism (from a craft shop or buy a cheap clock and take it apart)
A piece of thick cardboard
A pair of compasses
Thick, bright paper in blue, orange and two shades of yellow
Calligraphy pens
Tracing paper
A pencil and a ruler
A craft knife and scissors
Masking tape
PVA (household) glue

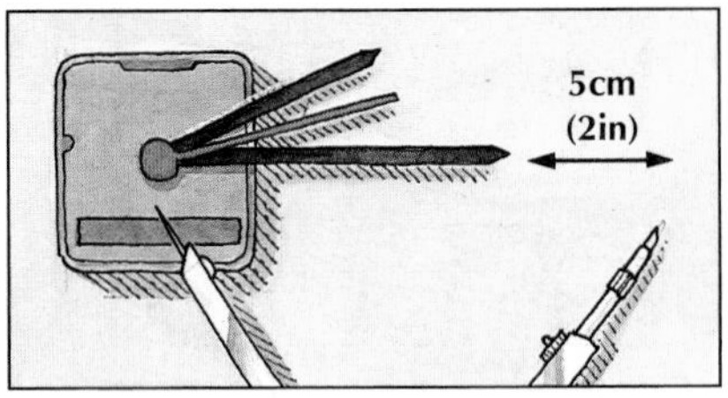

1. Open the compasses so that they are 5cm (2in) wider than the long hand of the clock. Draw a circle on the thick cardboard. Cut it out using a craft knife.

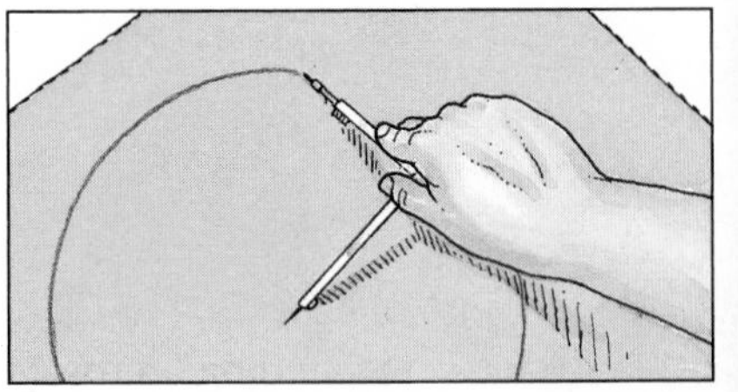

2. Draw a circle the same size as the cardboard on the dark yellow paper and on a piece of tracing paper. Use scissors to cut both of them out.

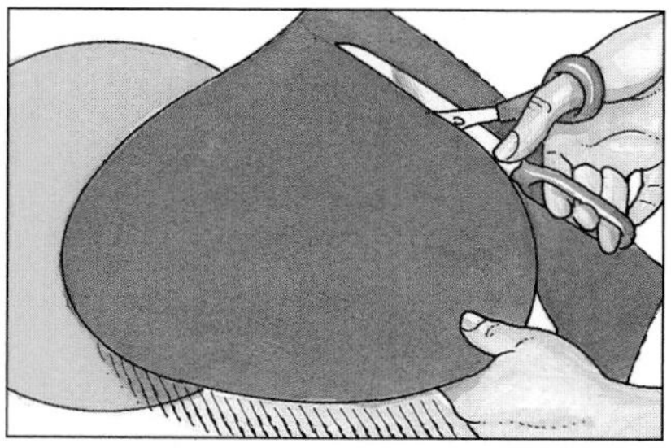

3. Reduce the width of the compasses by 8mm (3/8in) and draw a circle on the blue paper. Cut it out, using scissors.

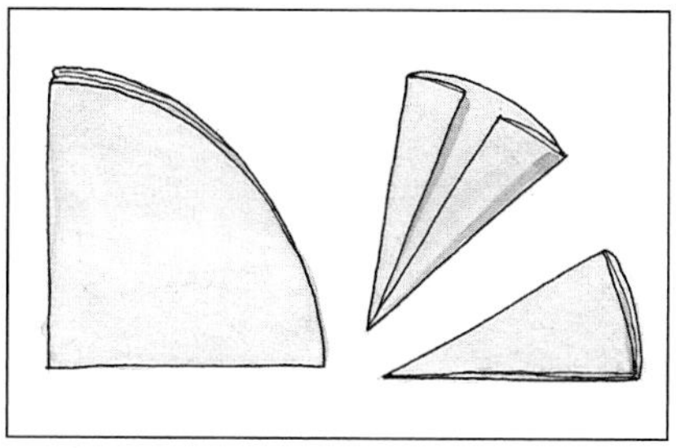

4. Fold the tracing paper into quarters. Then fold it into thirds by bending both edges in so that they overlap. Crease the folds.

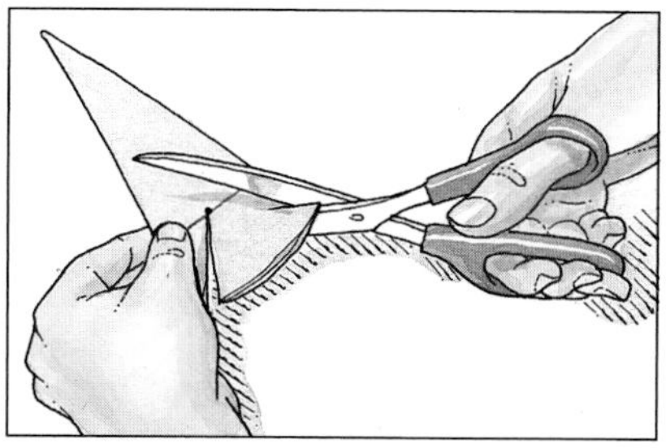

5. Draw a line 4cm (1 1/2in) from the edge of the circle. Make a mark halfway along this line. Cut in from both corners to this mark.

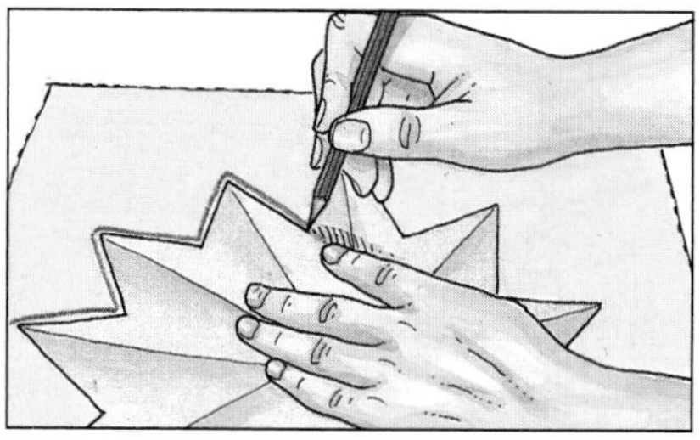

6. Open out the tracing paper and spread it out on the pale yellow paper. Draw around it, then use a ruler to straighten the lines. Cut out the star shape.

7. Set the compasses to 1cm (1/2in) wider than the short hand. Draw a circle on the dark yellow paper. Cut it out and put it in the middle of the star. Draw around it.

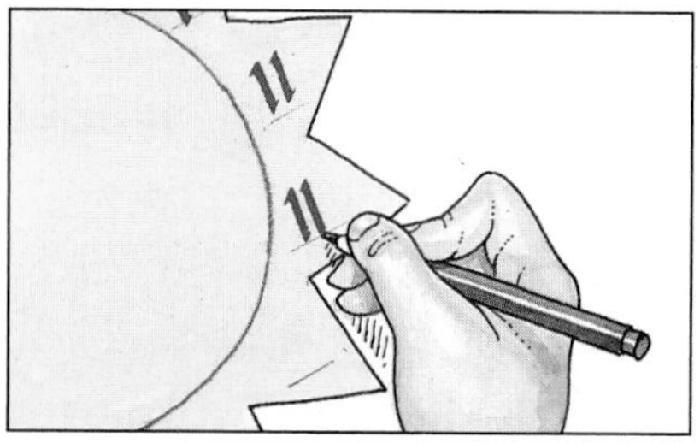

8. Each number fits on one of the points. Either draw them freehand, or try them out on tracing paper and then transfer them to the clock (see page 78).

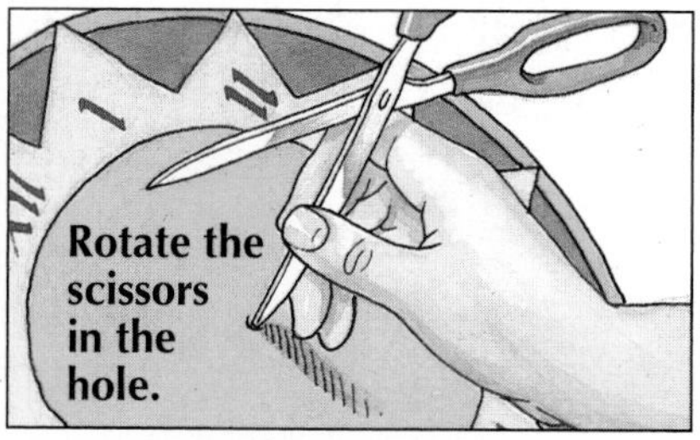
Rotate the scissors in the hole.

9. Glue the circles and the star to the cardboard, starting with the biggest one. Decorate the face (see below). Enlarge the central hole with some scissors.

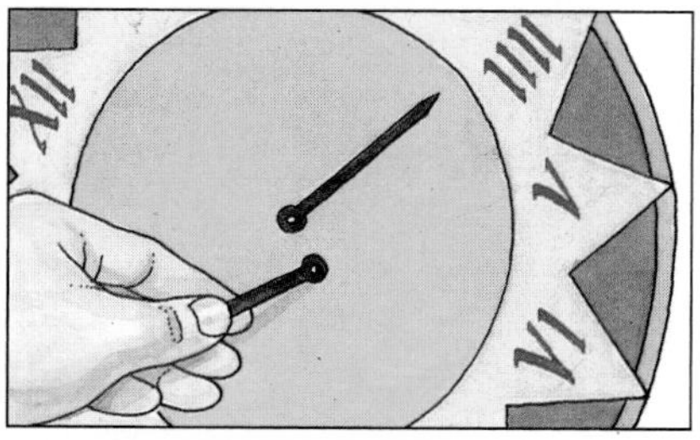

10. Take the hands off the clock mechanism. Push the spindle of the mechanism through the hole from the back. Replace the hands on the front of the clock.

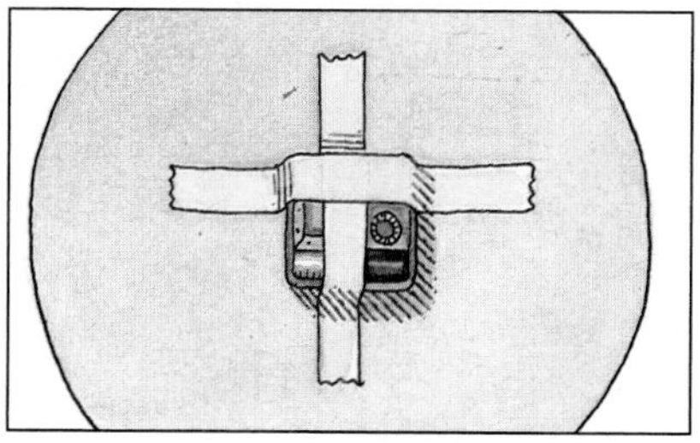

11. Attach the mechanism to the back of the clock with masking tape. If you want to make your clock more durable, paint it with a couple of coats of the glue.

Decorating the face

Make the face after attaching the circles and star in step 9. Begin by cutting an orange circle, the same size as the dark yellow one.

1. Draw in the features marked by the blue line. Cut them out carefully.

2. Glue the main part of the face and the left eye onto the yellow circle.

3. Turn over the pieces for the lips and cheek, and glue them in place.

Calligraphy on a plate

You will need:

A plain china plate
Ceramic paint which hardens in an oven (from a craft shop)
A pair of compasses
Tracing paper
A ballpoint pen
A black felt-tip pen
Double pencils (see page 51)
Scissors and a craft knife
A sponge
An old plastic lid or paper plate
Old newspapers
Book-covering film

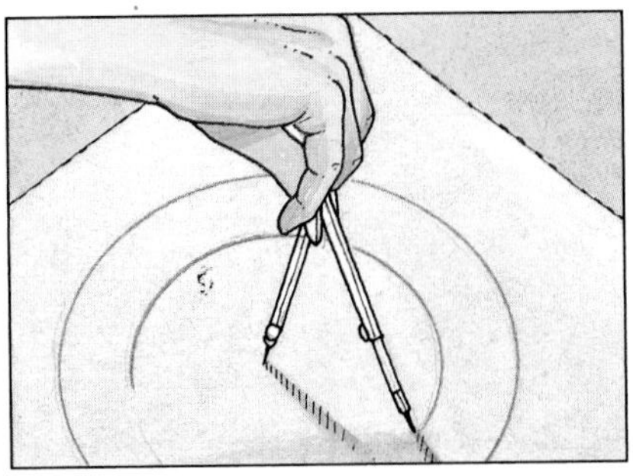

1. Draw around the china plate onto tracing paper. Draw in the rim of the plate by opening the compasses to half the width of the central area of the plate. Cut around the outline of the plate.

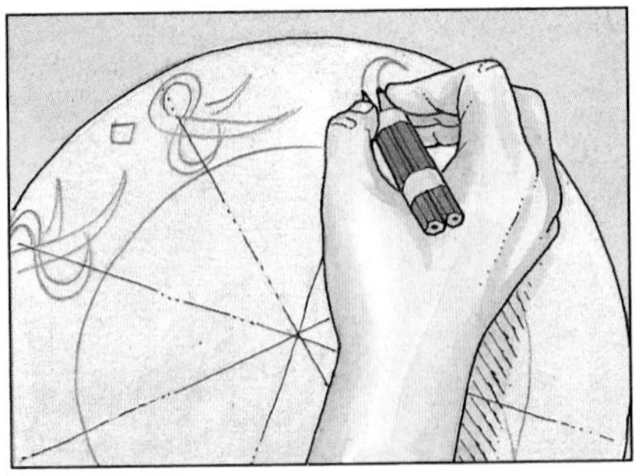

2. Fold the tracing paper into quarters and then in half again. Open it out. Using the creases as a guide for spacing, draw a pattern or lettering around the rim with double pencils.

To fill the inside shape of each bird, trace its outline onto tracing paper and cut it out. Place the tracing paper stencil on the plate and sponge through it.

The letter H was painted with a broad-edge brush.

3. On the tracing paper, draw carefully around your pencil lines with a black felt-tip pen. Make any of the thin parts of your pattern or lettering at least 3mm (1/8in) wide.

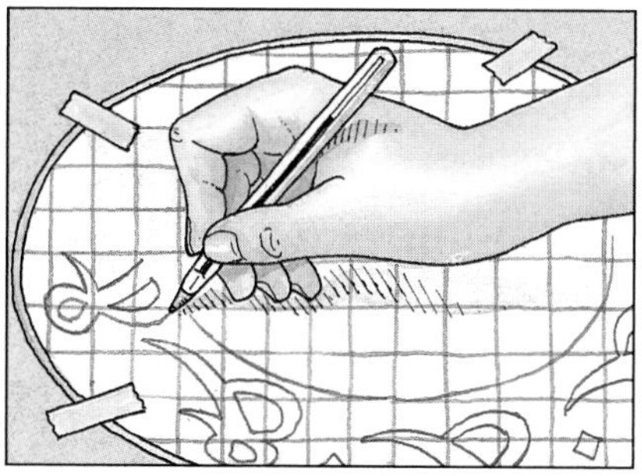

4. Draw around the plate on some book-covering film. Cut it out, then tape it over the tracing paper. Trace over your design using a ballpoint pen. Also draw the inner circle on the film.

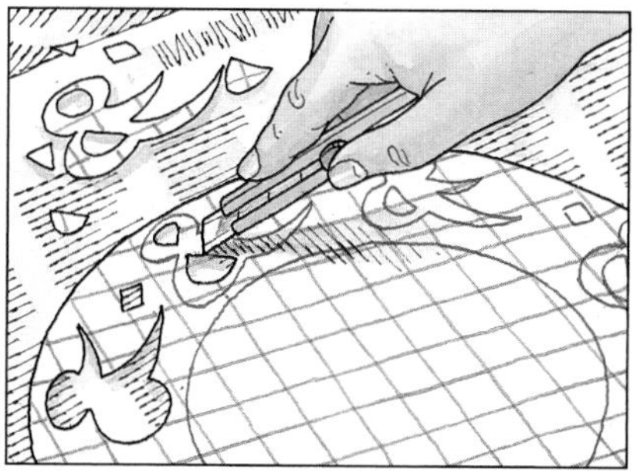

5. Place the book-covering film on a cutting surface (see page 79). Use a craft knife to cut out around the black lines that form your pattern or lettering. Keep all the shapes you have cut out.

Scratch fine lines with a cocktail stick, when the paint is still tacky.

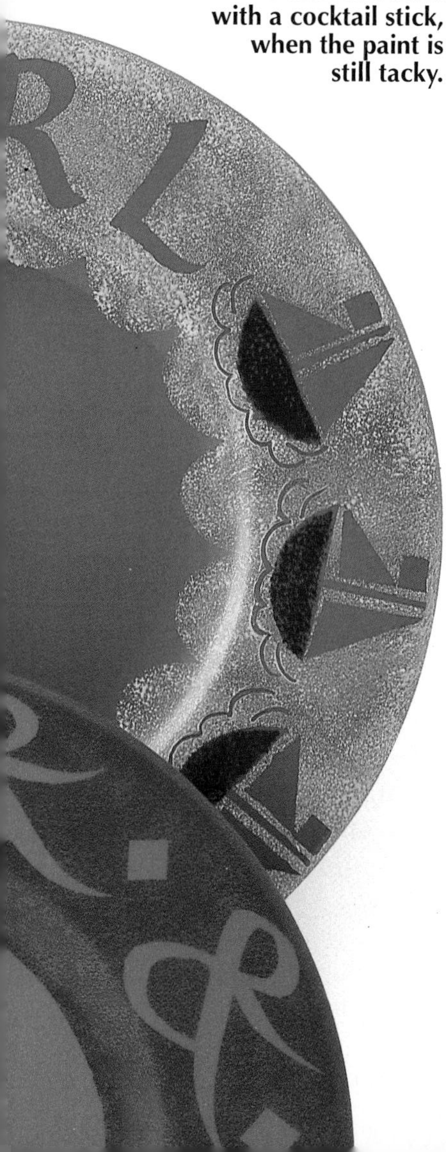

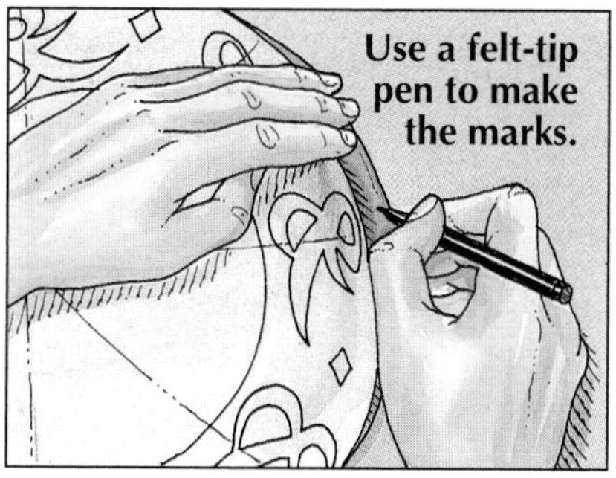
Use a felt-tip pen to make the marks.

6. Place your tracing paper over the plate and make a tiny mark at each crease. One by one, peel the backing paper off each shape and stick it onto the rim, using the marks as a guide.

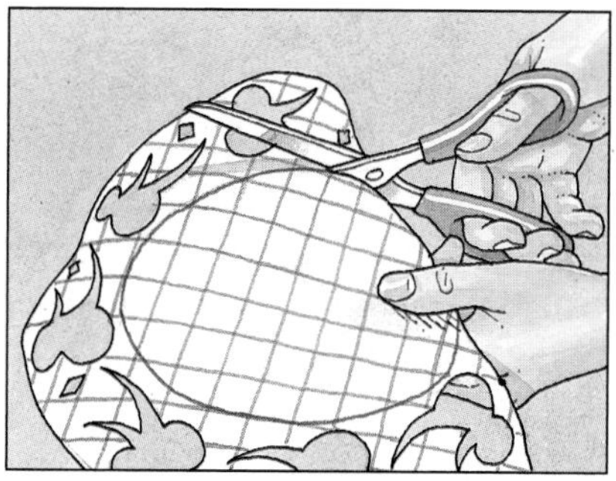

7. Use scissors to cut out the central circle from the book-covering film. Peel the backing paper off the circle and stick it very carefully in the middle of the plate.

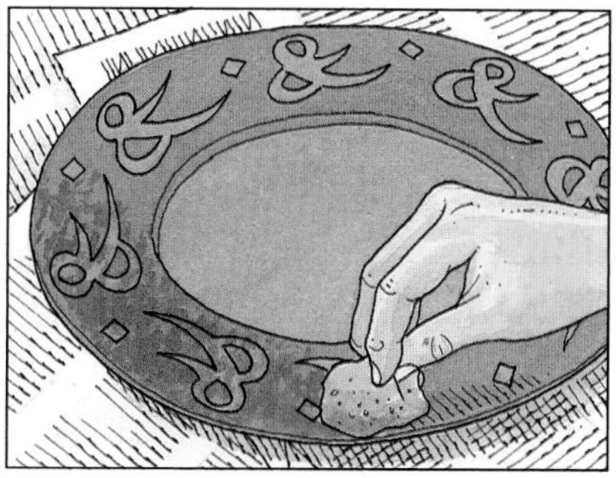

8. Put a little ceramic paint on the plastic lid. Dip the sponge into it and dab it onto some newspaper to get rid of excess paint. Dab the sponge lightly all over the rim of the plate.

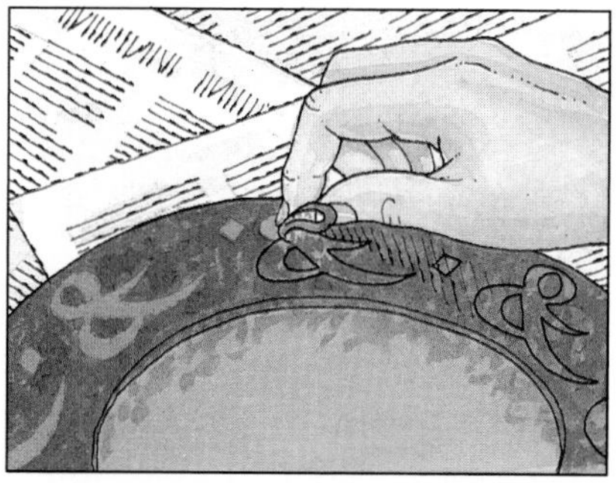

9. When the paint is still tacky, carefully peel off the film. It may help to slip the blade of a craft knife under it to start it off. Follow the maker's instructions for hardening the paint.

An address book

You will need:

4 pieces of fairly thick paper 20 x 30cm (8 x12in)
2 sheets of contrasting bright paper 20 x 30cm (8 x 12in)
Thick bright paper 20 x 30cm (8 x 12in) for the cover
A craft knife
A ruler and pencil
75cm (30in) of embroidery thread and a large needle
Calligraphy pens
Glue and masking tape

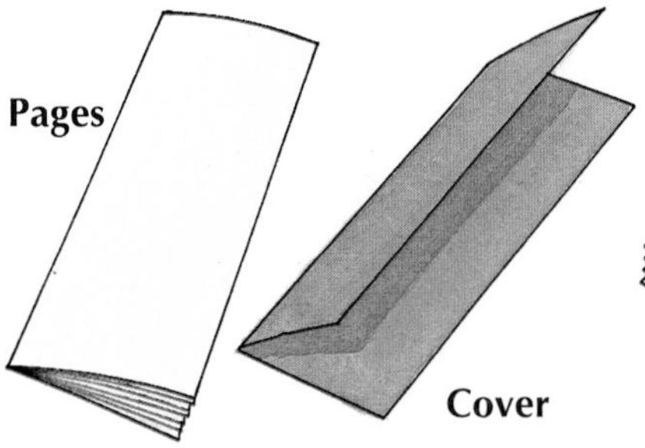
Pages
Cover

1. Fold the four sheets of thick paper in half. Place the pages inside each other to make a book. Score a line down the middle of the cover and fold it.

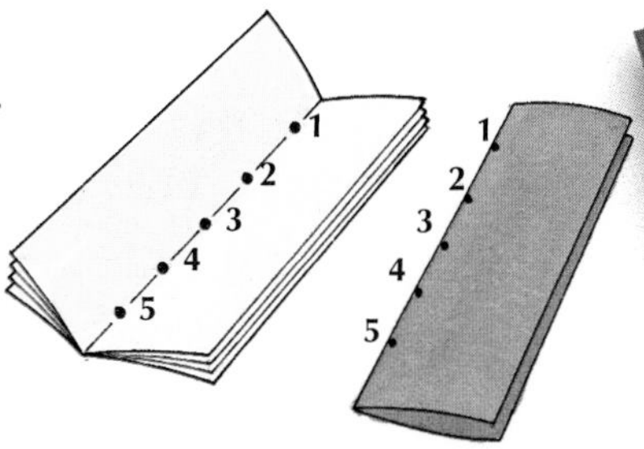
1
2
3
4
5
1
2
3
4
5

2. On the inside piece of paper make five light pencil marks at 5cm (2in) intervals along the fold. Do the same on the cover paper and number the marks.

3. Stitching the pages together

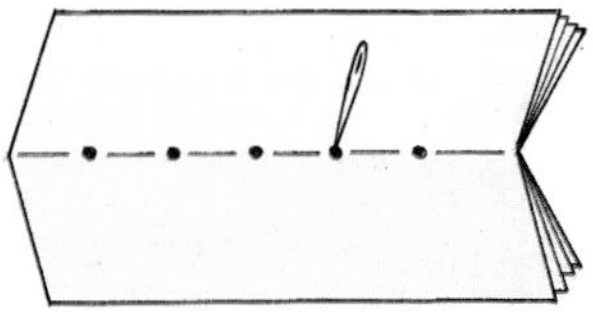

a) Push the needle through the pages at each mark on the fold.

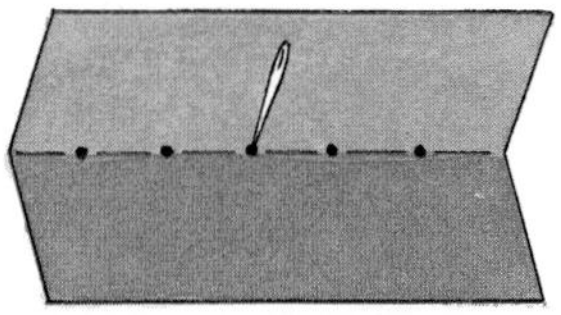

b) Do the same with the cardboard and put it around the pages.

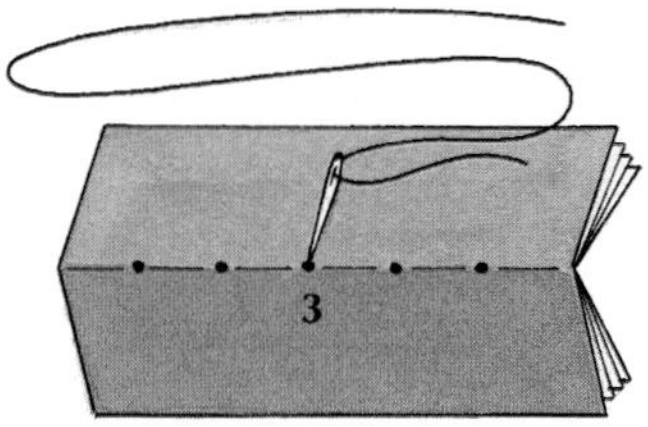
3

c) Thread the needle and push it through the book at hole 3.

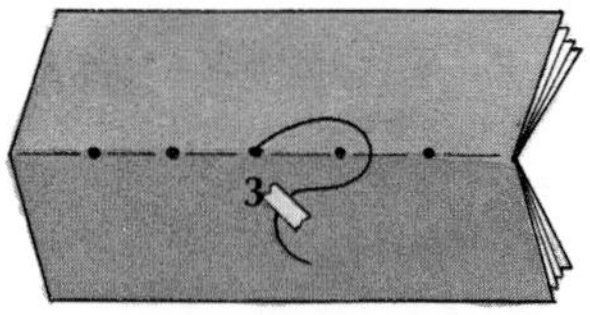
3

d) Leave about 20cm (8in) loose. Secure it with a little tape.

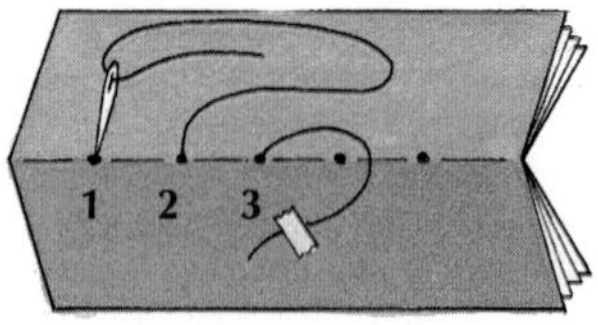
1 2 3

e) Push the needle up through hole 2 and down through 1.

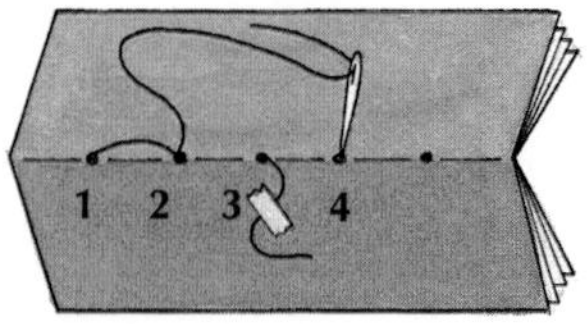
1 2 3 4

f) Stitch back up through 2 and down through 4.

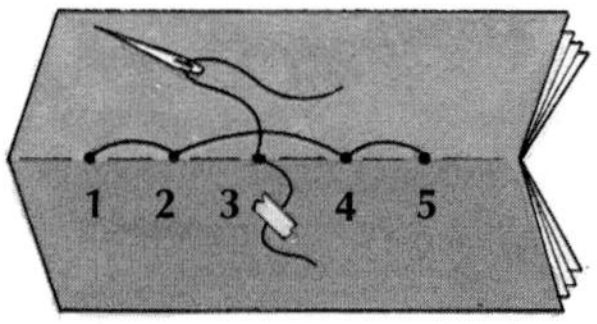
1 2 3 4 5

g) Stitch up through 5, down through 4 and up through 3.

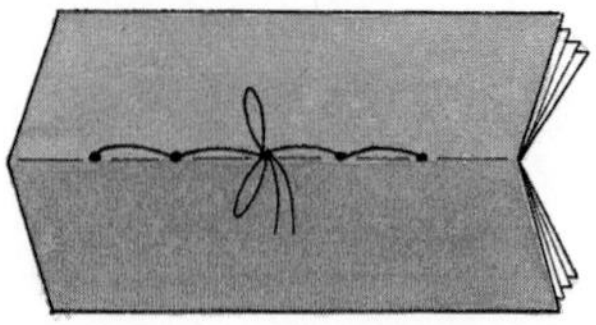

h) Tie the loose ends tightly in a double knot and trim the ends.

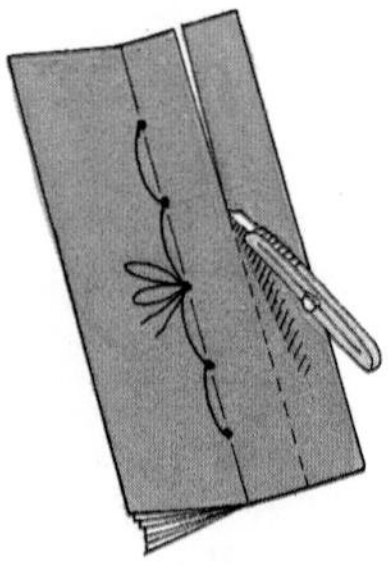

Fold back the back cover and pages so that you don't cut through them.

4. On the front cover, draw a line 5.5cm (2¼in) from the fold, then cut along the line, using a craft knife. Be careful that you don't cut the pages.

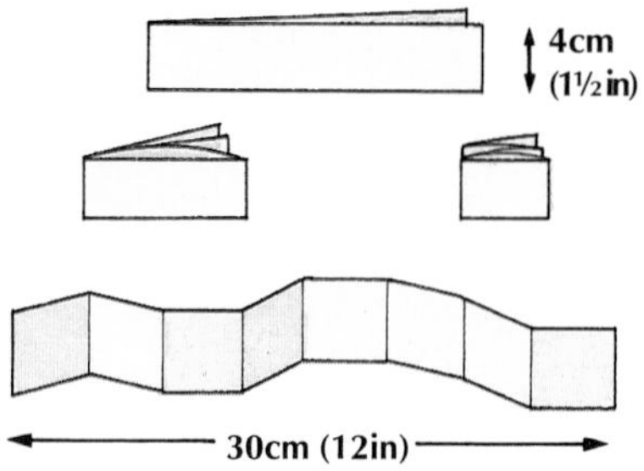
4cm
(1½in)
30cm (12in)

5. Cut a strip of rough paper 30 x 4cm (12 x 1½in). Fold it in half three times to give eight equal sections. This will act as a guide for the decorated sections.

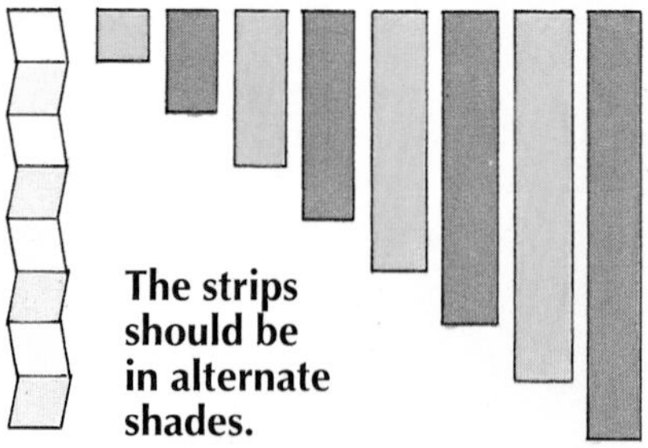
The strips should be in alternate shades.

6. Cut strips of bright paper 5 x 30 cm (2 x 12in). Using the guide, cut one section from one paper and two sections from the other, and so on.

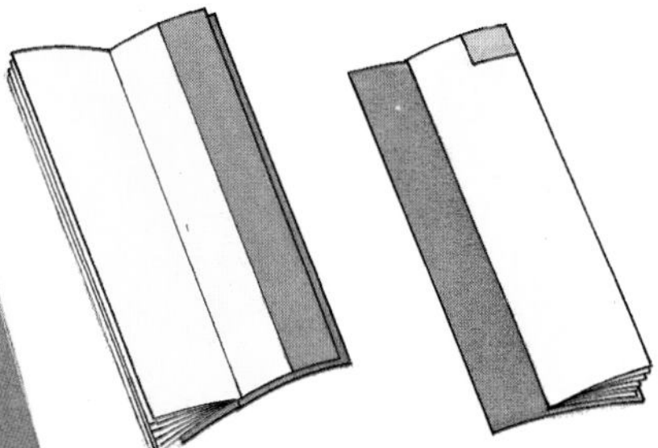

7. Stick the longest strip of bright paper onto the last page in the book. Stick the next longest onto the next page, and so on.

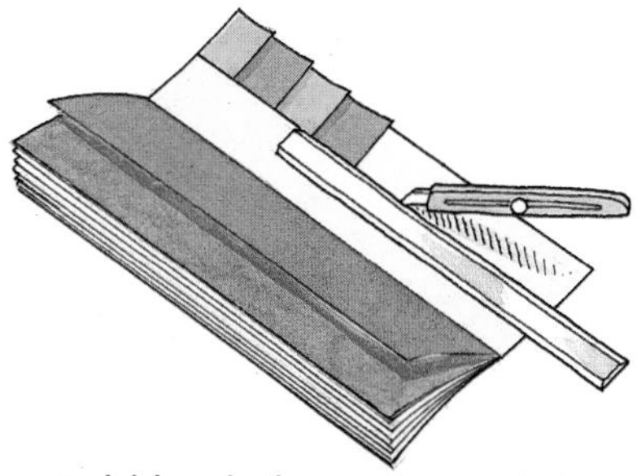

8. Fold back the cover and the rest of the pages in turn, so you can cut away the excess white paper at the bottom of each strip using a craft knife and a ruler.

You could print a pattern on the cover with a rubber stamp (see pages 58-59), or cut out the word "ADDRESSES" from a contrasting shade and glue it on.

Decorating the pages

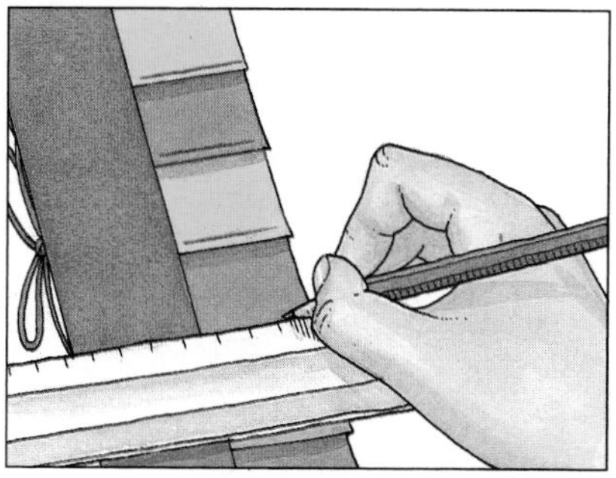

Draw faint pencil lines at the bottom of each strip for the position of the letters. On rough paper, try out different styles of lettering to fill the spaces.

The 2 longest strips will be STUV and WXYZ, the other strips have 3 letters each.

Use a calligraphy pen to write the letters directly onto the strips, or use tracing paper to transfer your letters (see page 78), then fill them in.

A calligraphy nightshirt

You will need:

A large T-shirt
A large sheet of paper
Fabric paint from a craft shop
Clear book-covering film
A small sponge and a saucer
Masking tape and a craft knife
A large piece of cardboard
Paper towels
A ballpoint pen
A black felt-tip pen
A broad calligraphy pen

How to prepare your T-shirt

The cardboard stops the paint from soaking through to the back.

If the T-shirt is new, wash it to remove any 'finish'. Iron it to remove any creases. Slide the cardboard inside the T-shirt.

Masking tape
Paper towels

Place some paper towels between the front of the T-shirt and the cardboard. Smooth the fabric and secure it to the cardboard using masking tape.

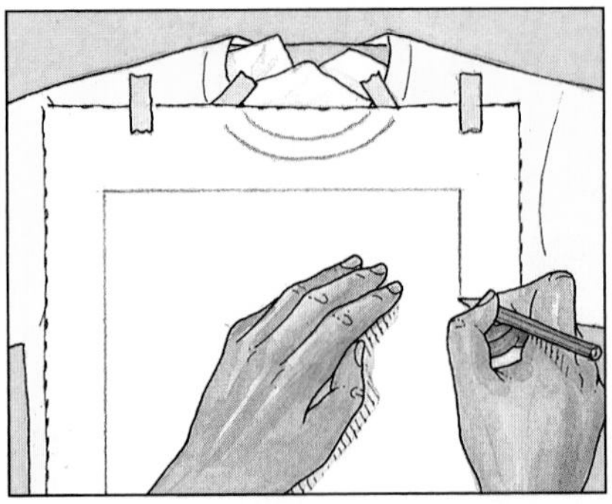

1. Spread the sheet of paper over the T-shirt and draw a rough outline of the area you want to decorate. Draw in the position of the arms and the neck.

!buenas no

2. Place the paper onto a flat surface. Design your stencil inside the outline. Use double pencils (see page 51) or a calligraphy pen for the lettering.

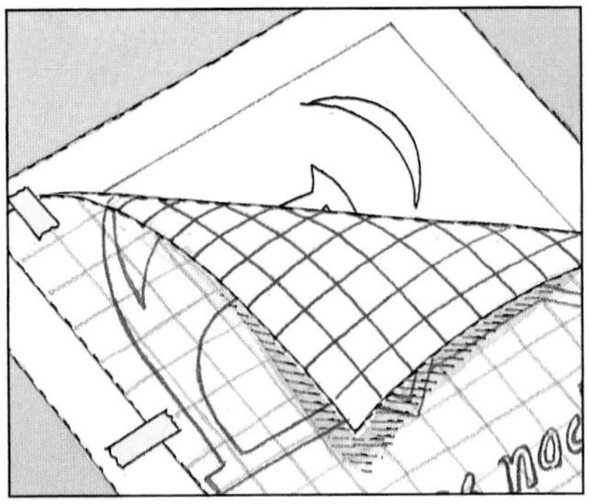

3. Outline your design with a black felt-tip pen. Tape a piece of book-covering film over the whole design, then draw over the lines with a ballpoint pen.

4. Put the film onto a cutting surface. Cut around each letter or shape and remove the pieces to leave a stencil. Keep any middle pieces of letters.

¡buenas noches!

5. Peel the backing paper away from the film at the top. Stick it in place on the T-shirt. Gradually peel the rest of the backing away, sticking it down as you do it.

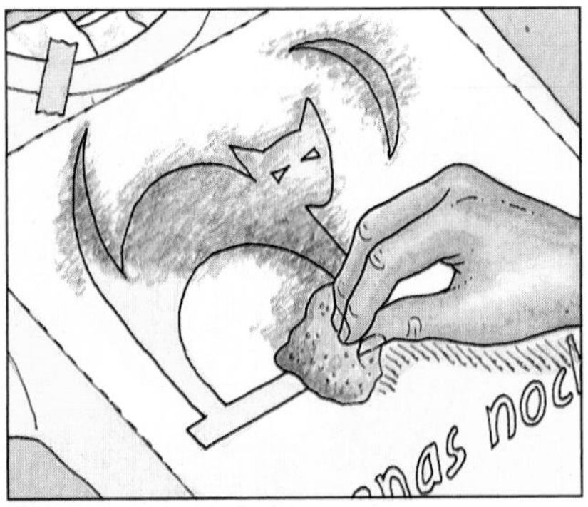

6. Pour some of the fabric paint onto a saucer. Dip the sponge into the paint and then gradually dab it all over the holes in your stencil to fill them in.

This T-shirt is decorated with small, intricate lettering. It is much easier to use large letters and simple shapes, as they are easier to cut out.

You could use the same method to print the name of a sport's team or club onto a T-shirt.

Draw a design to stencil onto boxer shorts or cycling shorts to wear with the nightshirt (see below right).

See page 21 for a different method of writing a message on a T-shirt

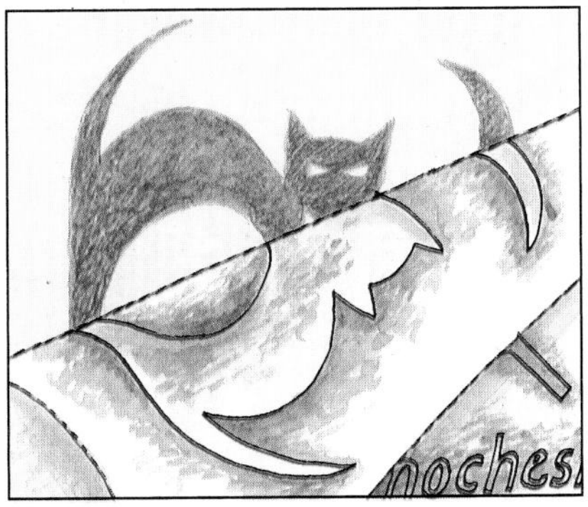

7. Leave the paint to dry thoroughly before peeling off the stencil. Follow the maker's instructions for 'fixing' the paint, so that the T-shirt can be washed.

Matching shorts

You could also decorate a pair of cycling shorts or boxer shorts in the same way as the T-shirt. Place the shorts onto a piece of paper and draw around them. Draw a design which fits onto the legs of the shorts. Follow the instructions from step 3.

A papier mâché bowl

Papier mâché takes quite a long time to do, but you do not need to do all the stages of sticking on the layers at one time. It also takes several days to dry out, but the results are worth waiting for.

You will need:

A large bowl
Newspaper cut into squares of about 4-5cm (1½-2in)
A small plastic container
Petroleum jelly
Artist's acrylic paints
PVA (household) glue
Emulsion paint
A thick and a fine paint brush
Carbon paper
Tracing paper
Masking tape
Self-adhesive labels
A sponge
A pair of scissors

1. Smear the inside of the bowl with an even layer of petroleum jelly to stop the newspaper from sticking to the bowl.

The tinted glue will help you to see each completed layer.

2. In a small container, mix six tablespoons of glue with two tablespoons of water. Tint the glue with a little acrylic paint.

Overlapping squares around the rim will be cut off later.

3. Lay squares of newspaper all over the greased surface of the bowl. Make sure they overlap each other slightly.

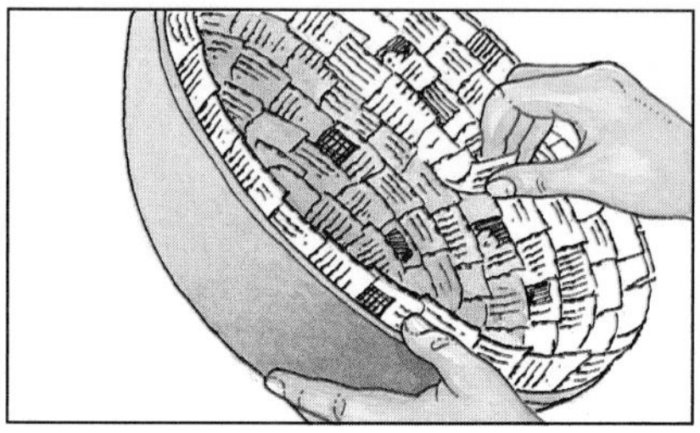

4. Paint the glue mixture gently over the surface and add another layer of squares. Overlap the rim of the bowl by about 3cm (1¼in).

Decorating the inside

1. Cut out simple shapes from self-adhesive labels. Peel off the backing paper and stick them on at regular intervals.

2. Put some acrylic paint on a saucer. Press the sponge into it and dab the paint over the shapes and the inside.

3. As soon as you have finished sponging on the paint, carefully remove the self-adhesive shapes.

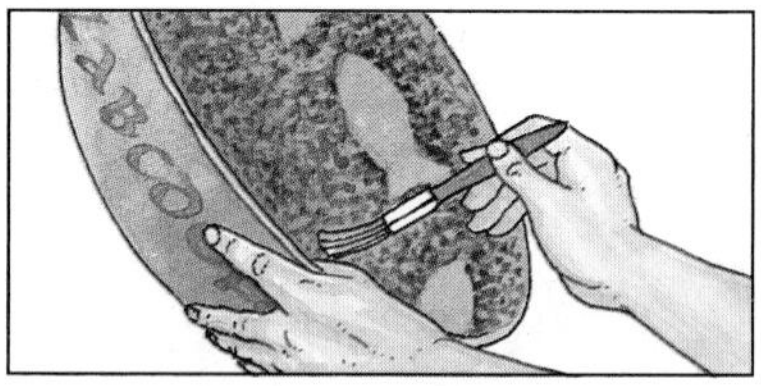

4. Paint the inside of the bowl with two coats of the glue. Allow each coat to dry before painting on the next one.

Add extra layers on the base to stop the bowl from toppling over.

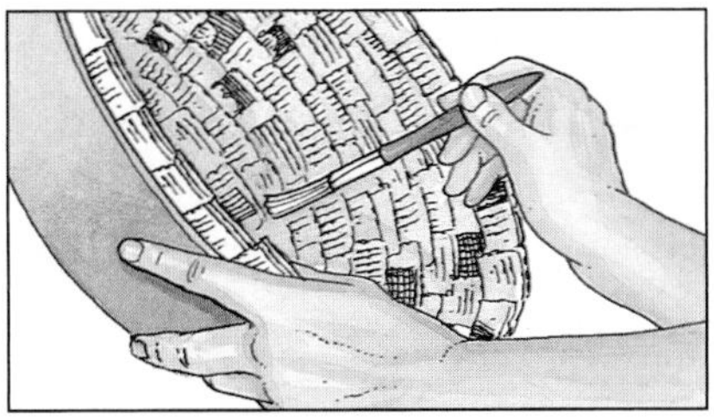

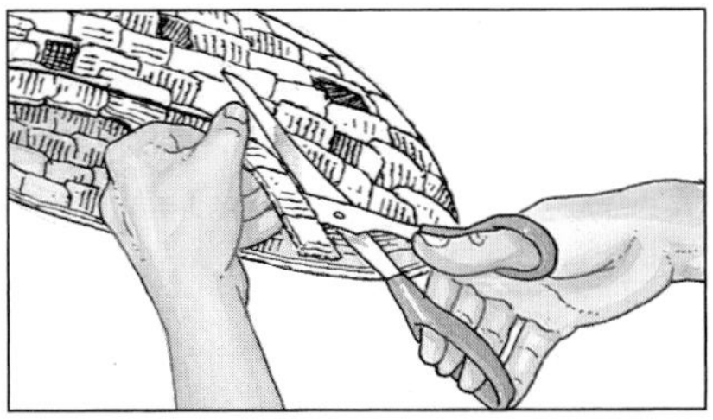

5. Add at least twelve more layers of glue and newspaper to make the bowl strong. Continue to overlap the rim with each layer.

6. Paint a final layer of glue on the inside of the bowl. Leave it in a warm place for two to three days to dry out completely.

7. Draw a line around the top of the original bowl, then ease out the papier mâché bowl and use scissors to cut around the line.

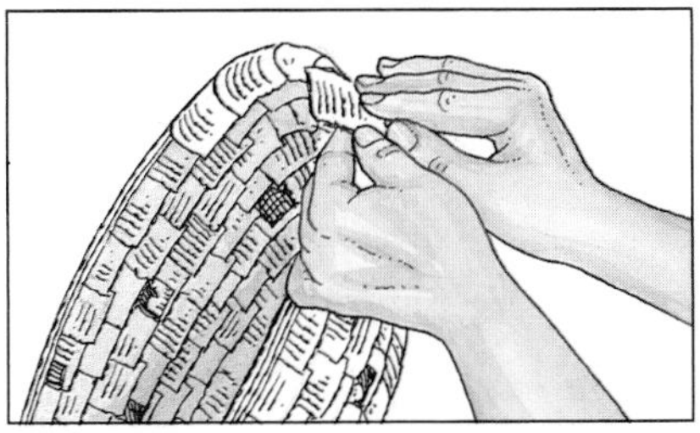

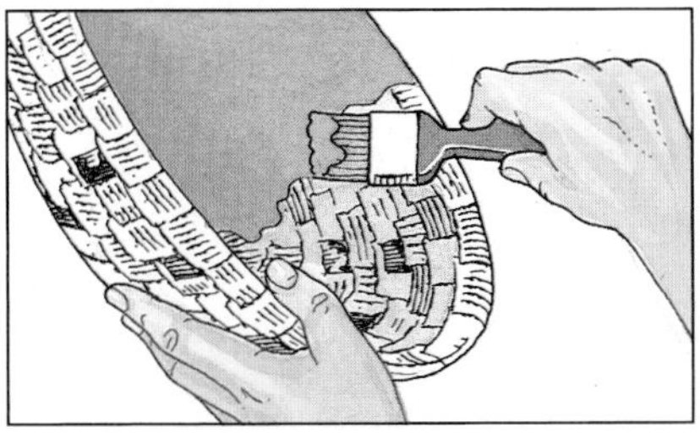

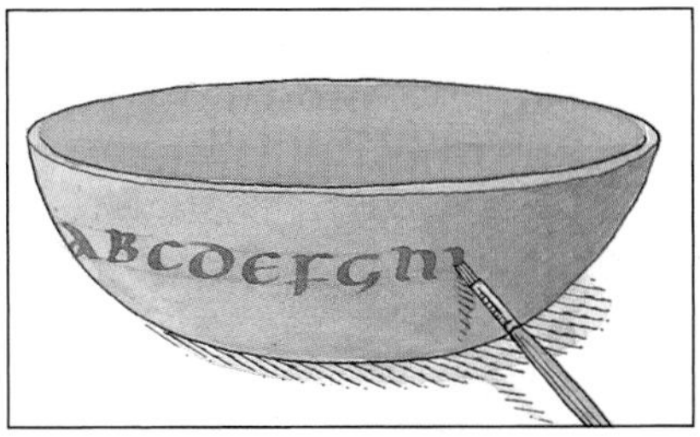

8. Stick squares over the rim to finish off the edge. Add a final layer of squares on the outside to make a smooth surface.

9. When dry, paint the inside of the bowl with emulsion paint, using the large brush. When this has dried, paint the outside.

10. Follow the instructions on page 63 to calculate the spacing of the letters on the outside of the bowl. Use acrylic paint for the lettering. Varnish with two coats of glue, allowing it to dry in between.

You cannot wash the bowl, but you can wipe it with a damp cloth to clean it.

Calligraphy and craft techniques

On these two pages you will find most of the techniques which are used in the projects.

Letter height

The width of your pen nib will determine the height of your letters (see page 10). The small diagram at the beginning of the each alphabet on pages 42-43, shows you its x-height. To find the x-height for the nib you are using, hold your pen nib at 90° and make small steps, one above the other. Remember to leave enough room in betwen your guidelines for your ascenders and descenders (see page 10).

An x-height of five nib widths.

Ascender

Descender

Measure guidelines using a ruler and a pencil so that the letters, ascenders and descenders are the same height.

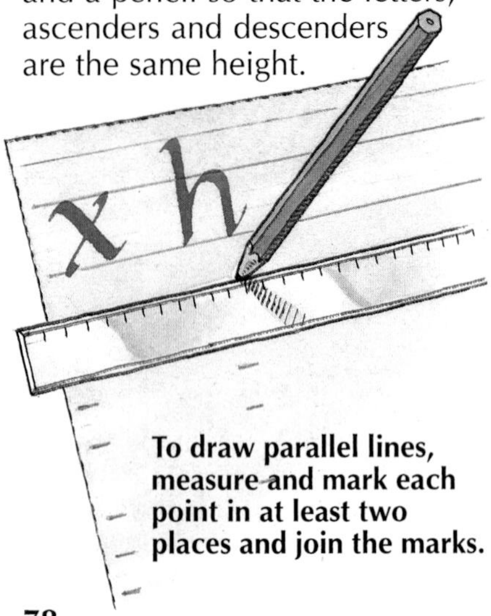

To draw parallel lines, measure and mark each point in at least two places and join the marks.

Spacing

Because letters are different shapes, the spaces between them cannot be measured exactly. Judge the spacing by eye so that it looks even. It's a good idea to try out your lettering on a piece of scrap paper before you work on any object. When you are happy with the spacing, trace over the lettering and transfer it to your object (see below).

If you are using large lettering, draw each letter separately, cut them out and stick them in place.

If your letters are small, leave a gap between each word the width of a letter 'o' in that alphabet.

Tracing

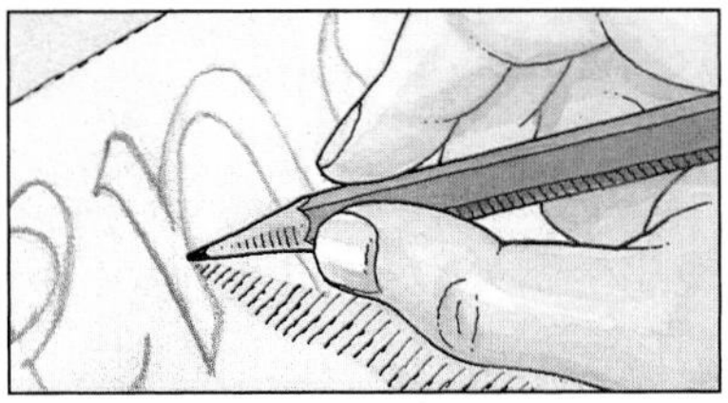

Once you have found the right spacing for your letters or words, trace around the outline of each letter with a pencil.

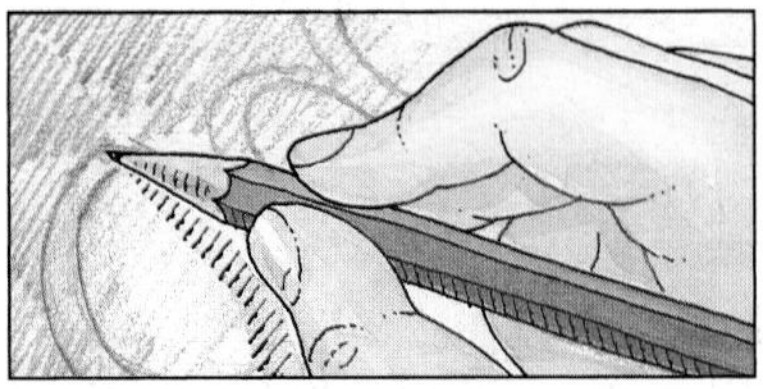

Scribble over the back of the lettering with a soft pencil, such as a B or 2B pencil.

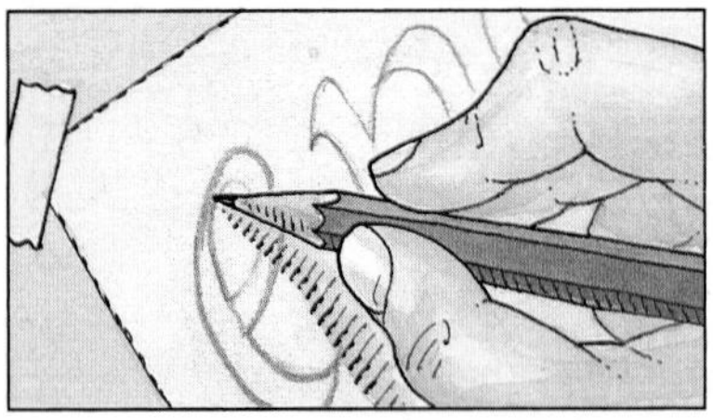

Turn the tracing paper over and secure it in position with masking tape. Trace over the letters with a hard 2H pencil.

You can use carbon paper to transfer your lettering. This technique is described fully in the terracotta pot project (see pages 66-67). Dressmakers' carbon paper is best to use because it isn't inky or messy.

If you are going to use a brush to fill in the lettering, draw the outlines of the letters.

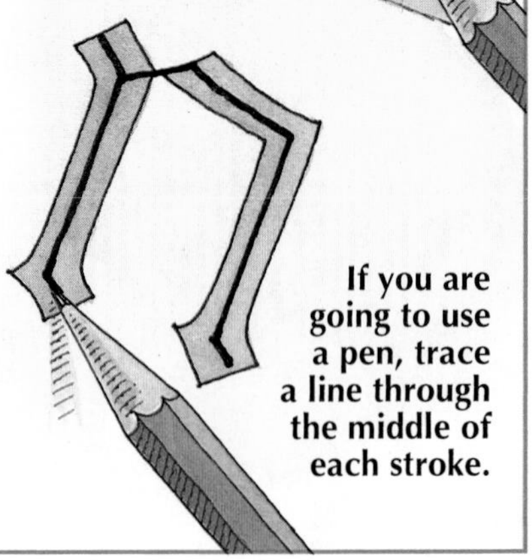

If you are going to use a pen, trace a line through the middle of each stroke.

Layout

The way lettering is arranged on an object is called layout. To place a word centrally, do the lettering on a rough piece of paper. Fold the paper in half to find the middle and trace or copy it onto your object.

If the word is too long for a space, use a narrower nib and make the lettering smaller.

Line up lettering to the left or right by cutting words into strips and taping them in position. Then, trace or copy them onto an object.

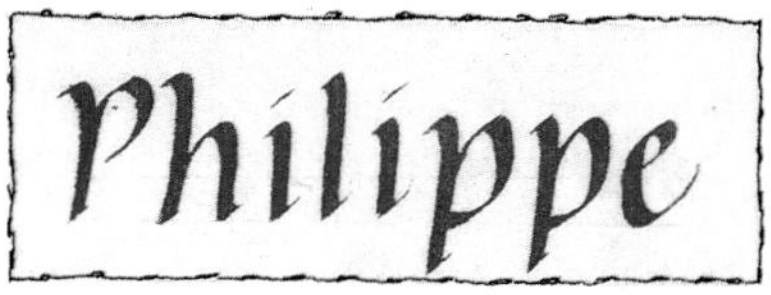

If a word doesn't fill a space, use a thicker nib and make the letters larger.

Folding paper and cardboard

Lightly fold the paper over, then run the bowl of a clean spoon along the fold to make a crease. To avoid marking your paper, place a piece of thin paper over the fold, then make the crease.

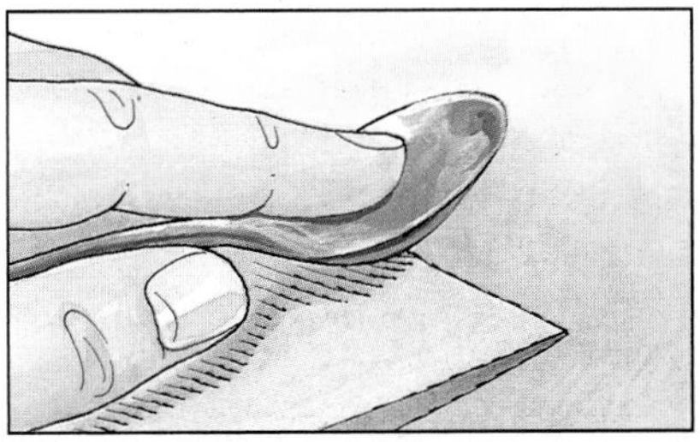

When folding cardboard or thick paper, it is best to score a line to fold along. Put a metal ruler along the line you wish to score, then run a craft knife along it very lightly. Do not cut into the cardboard or paper at all.

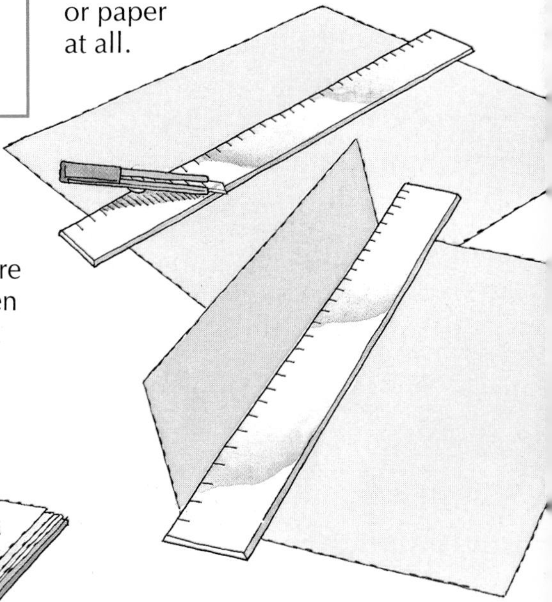

When you have scored a line, fold the cardboard or paper along the line. It may help to hold a ruler along the scored line as you make the fold.

Using a craft knife

Always take special care when using a craft knife. Make a cutting surface using very thick cardboard or several old magazines to avoid cutting into the surface below. Try to cut away from the fingers which are holding the paper steady. When cutting a straight line, it is best to use a metal ruler.

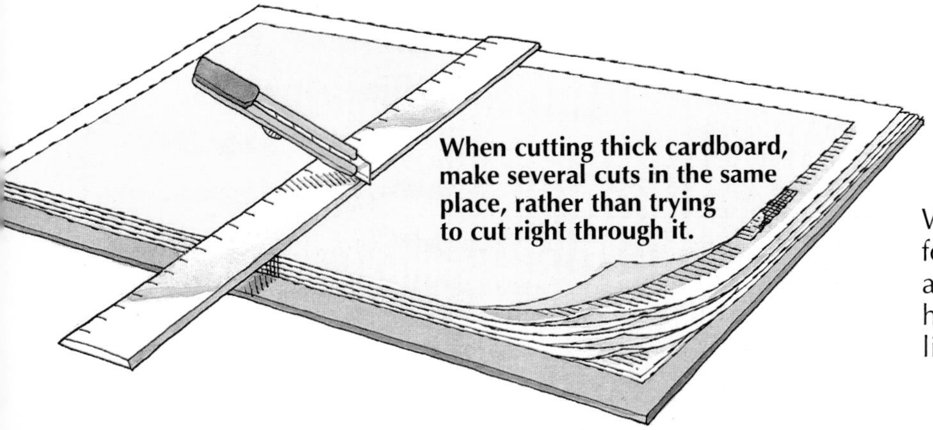

When cutting thick cardboard, make several cuts in the same place, rather than trying to cut right through it.

Index

address book 72-73
alphabets - Ancient Greeks 3
- Carolingian 2, 42
- Chinese 3, 27
- Foundational 3, 11, 30, 43
- Gothic 3, 10, 16, 17 22, 40
- Italic 3, 18, 19, 22, 30, 39, 41
- Phoenician 3
- Roman 2, 8, 9, 18, 22, 37, 40
- Rustics 2
- Uncials 2, 12, 30
- Versals 2, 20, 21, 41
angel decoration 64-65
ascenders 10, 12, 16, 18, 43, 46, 78
automatic pens 28, 42, 43

backgrounds 29, 33
basic shape 10, 18, 30, 46
birthday book 56-57
book cover 36, 53
books (for reference) 47
borders 22, 45
bowls 63, 76-77
brushes - calligraphy 28, 43, 50
- Chinese 26, 27, 45
built-up letters 20, 46
burnishing 23, 46

capitals - Gothic 16, 40
- Italic 18, 41
- Roman 2, 8, 9, 18, 22, 37, 40
- Rustic 2
- skeleton 8, 9
- Swash 18, 41
- Versals 20, 21, 41
cards 9, 24, 54-55, 64-65
careers information 38, 39
Carolingian miniscules 2, 42
ceramic paint 62, 63, 70, 71
certificate 17, 38
Chinese calligraphy 3, 26, 27, 45
clay (tiles) 37
clock 68-69
collage 35
colored ink 32
craft knife (using) 79
cross-hatching 22, 46
cut and paste 15, 19, 44, 46, 78

decorations 18, 21, 22, 23
descenders 10, 12, 16, 18, 46, 78
dip pens 6, 50
double pencils 51, 58, 62, 66, 70, 74
drawing board 4, 26, 29, 33, 39

embossing 36, 46, 52-53
enamel paint 37
equipment 4, 5, 6, 50

fabric paint 21, 74
family tree 12
felt-tip pens 5, 23, 50
flourish 18, 46
folder 19
Foundational 3, 11, 30, 43
fountain pens 6, 19, 50

gift boxes 60-61
gift tags 35, 58
giftwrap 34, 58-59
gilding 23, 46
gold 23
Gothic 3, 10, 16, 17, 22, 40
gouache 21, 23, 32, 33, 54
greetings cards 9, 24, 54-55, 64-65
guidelines 9, 11, 46, 78

handwriting 3, 19, 42
Hebrew calligraphy 47

illumination 22, 23, 46
illustration 13, 22, 27
incising (letters) 2, 37, 46
inks - colored 23, 50
- non-waterproof 5
ink stick 26
ink stone 26
invitations 13, 36
Islamic calligraphy 47
Italics 3, 18, 19, 22, 30, 39, 41

layout 14, 15, 46, 79
left-handed nibs 6, 51
logos 31, 46

majuscules 8
margins 14, 15, 46
masking fluid 33, 59
minuscules 2, 10, 46
mistakes 7, 9, 25
mugs 62-63

nibs 5, 6, 7, 13, 28, 30, 50, 51
numbers 45, 68

paper (types of) 4, 17, 24
paints - ceramic 62, 63, 70, 71
- enamel 37
- fabric 21, 74
- gouache 21, 23, 32, 33, 54
- watercolor 21, 33
pen illustration 22
pens - automatic 28, 42, 43
- dip pens 6, 50
- fountain pens 6, 19, 50
- homemade 5, 29, 59
- problems 7
plates 70-71
portfolio 38, 46, 47
poster 5, 35

quills 28, 47

Roman capitals 2, 8, 9, 18, 22, 37, 40
rubber stamps 31, 54, 58-59
rubbings 35, 46
ruling up 9, 11, 46, 78
Rustics 2

sans serif 9, 39, 40, 46
serifs 9, 18, 20, 37, 40, 46
skeleton letters 8, 10, 46
spacing 9, 78
spattering 33
stationery 31, 36, 38, 52, 53
stencils 22, 34, 46, 62-63, 70-71, 74-75
swashes 18, 30, 41

T-shirts 21, 74-75
techniques (for projects) 78-79
terracotta pots 66-67
tracing 78

Uncials 2, 12, 30

Versals 2, 20, 21, 41

wash (color) 33, 46
watercolor paint 21, 33
wax crayon 5, 33, 35
weight (of letters) 13, 17, 30, 46

x-height 10, 11, 13, 30, 46, 78

No part of this publication may be reproduced in whole or in part, or stored in a retrieval system, or transmitted in any form or by any means, electronic, mechanical, photocopying, recording, or otherwise, without written permission of the publisher. For information regarding permission, write to Usborne Publishing Ltd., Usborne House, 83-85 Saffron Hill, London, EC1N 8RT, England.

First published in Great Britain in 1994 by Usborne Publishing Ltd. • ISBN 0-439-45707-6 •

Copyright © 1994 by Usborne Publishing Ltd. All rights reserved.

Published by Scholastic Inc., 557 Broadway, New York, NY 10012, by arrangement with Usborne Publishing Ltd.

The name Usborne and the devices are trademarks of Usborne Publishing Ltd. SCHOLASTIC and associated logos are trademarks and/or registered trademarks of Scholastic Inc.

12 11 10 9 8 7 6 5 4 • 5 6 7/0 • Printed in the U.S.A. • 40 • First Scholastic printing, November 2002